FIREWATER
and
FORKED TONGUES

A Sioux Chief Interprets
U. S. History

by
M. I. McCREIGHT

Illustrations by
CHARLES M. RUSSELL

TRAIL'S END PUBLISHING CO., INC.
Authentic Western Material

725 Michigan Boulevard
Pasadena 10, California

FIRST EDITION
1947

Printing Statement:

Due to the very old age and scarcity of this book, many of the pages may be hard to read due to the blurring of the original text, possible missing pages, missing text and other issues beyond our control.

Because this is such an important and rare work, we believe it is best to reproduce this book regardless of its original condition.

Thank you for your understanding.

WHEN THE TRAIL WAS LONG BETWEEN CAMPS

BY CHARLES M. RUSSELL

"It is greatly to be wished that some competent person would write a full and true history of our national dealings with the Indians. Undoubtedly the latter have suffered terrible injustice at our hands."

—THEODORE ROOSEVELT.

Contents

Contents *(Continued)*

Illustrations

Publisher's Preface

The knowledge that there existed the manuscript material embodied in this book came as a surprise late in 1946. From the first reading it was evident that here was a priceless gem that had been fused by an ardent student of the Indian and a lover of fair play.

M. I. McCreight (now in his eighty-second year) had gone west as a boy, and had seen the Indian reduced to beggary through the ruthless treatment of his conquerors. The fires lit in his heart and mind during those years remained with him. All during an active business life in Pennsylvania he kept in touch with his Indian friends — studied avidly everything he could find on the subject of their history (too often slanted from the white man's viewpoint). He sifted and combed his extensive library until he had a fine knowledge of the subject. Interspersed with his active life and studies he found time to travel back over the West that he'd known as a lad, and to renew old friendships and make new ones among the Indians.

Indians do not readily take their traditional enemy into their confidence, but gradually several old chiefs, largely of the Sioux tribes, came to understand him. They called him "brother" and gave him the name Tchanta Tanka — Great Heart.

Thus it was that after many years he was able to entertain his friends of the West — Flying Hawk, American Horse, Lone Bear, Good Face, Plenty Coups, Iron Tail and others now gone to the Sand Hills. They came to visit at his home in DuBois, Pennsylvania, which he named the Wigwam. Here they found rest, a peaceful atmosphere, an understanding heart and a firm friend.

In this friendly atmosphere McCreight discovered what few white men have learned — that the Indian, without written books and paper-talk, had well defined ideas of United States history — many wholly contrary to the white man's books. This unwritten history had been handed down through the generations by the Chiefs and the medicine men of the tribe. It is likely to be more truthful than much of the white man's written history, for the Indian was basically more honest and forthright than were the men who robbed him of his home and his heritage.

And so it was that among his closest friends McCreight found Flying Hawk, the Sioux, to be a profound historian, statesman and philosopher. And by careful questioning and diplomacy he succeeded, over a period of years, in getting Flying Hawk to retell in his own way the history of this land — once the Indian's own — from the first coming of the white man.

Nor was this enough. The author exercised great care in assembling the material. After it was translated through an interpreter and typed it was read back to

Flying Hawk for his correction and approval. When Flying Hawk was satisfied and pronounced the paper-talk "washta" (good), the Sioux Chief signed each document with his thumb-print.

It is this material which is incorporated in this book and which we have reason to believe is worthy of earnest study by any American who is open-minded and wants to understand the Indian's viewpoint of our history. It is more than history, it is an insight into the clean, clear thinking and philosophy of the noble red man — for there were, and are, nobles in the ofttimes lowly hogans, wickiups and huts of the Indians of the United States of America.

Because this material was garnered over a long period of years in many interviews with Flying Hawk it would be impossible to arrange in chronological order; rather the thought has been to preserve the flavor of its original telling.

Excerpts from this manuscript have been privately published by the author in pamphlet form under the titles *Chief Flying Hawk's Tales* (1936) and *The Wigwam — Puffs from the Peace Pipe* (1943).

Flying Hawk was well qualified to act as historian of the Sioux. He was a youth when the white invasion of the Sioux country took place at the close of the Civil War. He was a nephew of Sitting Bull (his mother and Sitting Bull's wife were sisters). His full brother, Kicking Bear, had been a leader of the Ghost Dances. He had taken part as a lad in tribal wars with the Crows and the Piegans and he had fought alongside the Great Chief

Crazy Horse when Custer's command was wiped out on the Little Big Horn in 1876.

When the humdrum life in a two-room log cabin in the desolate Bad Lands country, enhanced by the economic pressure, became too confining for his restless spirit, Flying Hawk joined Buffalo Bill's Show, Colonel Miller's 101 Ranch Show and the Sells-Floto Circus, traveling throughout the country — after all, even an Indian had to eat! He died at Pine Ridge, South Dakota, December 24, 1931 — died in want, for he had written that his little band were saved from starvation only through contributions from Gutson Borglum and the Red Cross the year prior to his death.

H. E. BRITZMAN

TRAIL'S END
Pasadena, California
June 6, 1947

Foreword

The historic writings covered herein, largely the dictation of Chief Flying Hawk, a survivor of the Custer fight, are a faithful series of tales as known and handed down by the Sioux.

This old Chief lived through the serious times that befell our people following the gold discovery in the Black Hills; his experiences were of the most trying kind. Perhaps no other Indian of his day was better qualified to furnish reliable data covering the period of the great Sioux war, beginning with the ruthless exploitation by rum-sellers, prospectors and adventurers, of their homes and hunting grounds pledged to them forever by sacred treaty with the Government, and ending at the deplorable massacre of Wounded Knee.

My grandfather accompanied Flying Hawk's people and joined in the historic affair at Little Big Horn, and, as a consequence, in my boyhood days on the Lower Brule reservation and early life amongst my own people, the Sioux, I absorbed much of the Indian's view of the white man's one-sided history of the United States.

I have read the manuscript in preparation for this work, and unhesitatingly endorse it and recommend its publication, believing it will meet with full approval of every reader who cares to know and understand truth of our Indian problem.

I knew many of the characters mentioned in the work and I know the author, whom I regard as well qualified to put together this most interesting and instructive record.

(signed) OHITIKA

(Benjamin Brave)

Member of the Sioux Tribe

November, 1937

Introduction

Few are now living who mingled with the Sioux
Indians during their free and happy life on the northwestern prairies when the buffalo still furnished them
food and raiment, dwellings and warm robes for their
comfort in winter. Few now alive saw them in their villages among the trees at the border of some lake or river,
or in the wide-open flower-decked virgin plainsland.
Only there could the native Indian be seen and understood, for there was the home and natural environment
of the horse-Indians, the great Sioux tribe; there, too,
was the summer range of the buffalo.

We may read about them, see paintings and museum
figures to represent them; but we cannot go into the Old
West and visit them in their picturesque camps and see
the color and hear the sounds that emanated therefrom.
Gone forever are the charming teepees of painted buf-
falo-skins, fitted snugly to polished poles with antler-like
tips from which smoke curled lazily away; homes built
without regard to engineering plan, but wholly for util-
ity and momentary convenience; always graceful, har-
monious and attractive.

Picture in mind's eye the temporary homes of happy

housekeeping squaws, always busy with cooking, sewing, dressing skins, making beadwork for husbands and children or pemmican for winter stores; in their own white deer-skin waist and skirt and beaded moccasins, keeping the interiors of their lodges scrupulously clean and in order. Ponies graze about in luscious pasture, and children romp and play in mimic warfare or with rag dolls, shoot at gophers with tiny bows and arrows, or imitate their elders in tying small poles to the family dog for a travois to give the babe a ride.

The men are absent on a hunt; boys guard the grazing ponies. The Chief and old men confer on place for the next encampment; they stand erect with a lone eagle feather dangling from the hair, a painted robe draped over the shoulders, as only a Chief or Roman senator could wear with grace and dignity. Who has not seen this, has not seen Indians!

Flying Hawk was a youth when the white invasion of the Sioux country took place at the close of the Civil War and flowed into the great plains of the upper Missouri and the mountains of Montana, when gold was discovered there and in the Black Hills; it was the day of the real "Wild West" that he was born and grew to manhood. The region was a vast pastureland for the millions of buffalo which furnished the Indians food and clothing and shelter in abundance. His early life was romantic, and withal a happy one.

Youth and early manhood saw him leading tribal war-parties against the common enemy, the Crows. He was but fifteen when the trouble came with the white sol-

diers over the Government's disregard of sacred treaties;
he was active in nearly all the battles with United States
troops during the great Sioux war; he was with Crazy
Horse from the first to the last shot in wiping out Custer's
command on the Little Big Horn in 1876; he suffered
with his compatriots; saw his leaders assassinated —
Crazy Horse, Sitting Bull, Spotted Tail; and witnessed
his family and friends suffer from neglect, cheated by
dishonest Government agents, rum-peddlers and traders;
saw them die from starvation.

Flying Hawk's mature years were those in which the
Government wrote its darkest pages of United States
history — pages which all patriotic American citizens
now wish might be erased; and he died in want. During
the winter of 1930-1931 he wrote that his people were
saved from starvation only by contributions from Gutson
Borglum and emergency action by the Red Cross. Had
he received his just dues from funds owed his tribe from
the Government he would have been saved from this suffering, and might be alive today. He died in December,
1931.

Flying Hawk was born "about full moon of March,
1852," a few miles south of Rapid City, the son of Chief
Black Fox and Iron Cedarwoman. His mother and Sitting Bull's wife were sisters, thus he was the nephew of
the famous medicine man. Kicking Bear, the noted
hostile and a leader in the Ghost Dances led by Short
Bull, was his full brother. It was during the celebrating
of the coming of the New Christ, at the camp on Grand

River, that the cowardly and wholly uncalled-for murder of Sitting Bull occurred in 1890.

At the age of twenty-six, Flying Hawk married two sisters, White Day and Goes-Out-Looking; the latter wife bore him one son whom they named Felix. A cousin of these wives married James McLaughlin, who, for many years, was prominent as a representative of Government in Indian affairs, and who was agent at Standing Rock when Sitting Bull was killed; another cousin was wife of C. R. Jordon, prominent as a trader at Rosebud Agency.

It was when he was twenty-four that Flying Hawk and the great War Chief Crazy Horse led their clan in the Custer fight, where they were credited with special bravery, and perhaps more actual slaughter than any others in the battle. Together they followed and "got" the last man, whose body was later found nearly a half mile from where the men of the Custer command lay dead on the hot and dusty battlefield.

Flying Hawk became a Chief at the age of thirty-two.

The writer visited the homeland of the old Chief in 1928 to join the Indians in the ceremonies of the last Sun Dance. It was a sorrowful occasion for one who had lived with them half a century before, when they knew freedom, happiness and health. Only one who had known the Sioux before their herds of buffalo were exterminated, and their suffering through the long years thereafter, can understand and appreciate the enormity of the crime thus inflicted upon a great nation of innocent and helpless people. Their former wars with the United

States armies were merciful in comparison; their slow death from hunger and disease was inexcusable. Slavery of the imported blacks had been abolished long ago as an humanitarian act, but the real Americans, and original owners of the country, were made victims of every known rascally trick and subterfuge to take from them their homes and hunting grounds. Thus they were enslaved; and their bondage included constant hunger, slow starvation, demoralization, disease and death.

Flying Hawk came for his last visit at the Wigwam in 1929. He had been traveling with the circus, and the pony riding, war dances and inclement weather were weighing on his health at the age of seventy-seven. When met at the train he felt ill; he was taken to the doctor, who said he was threatened with pneumonia and must have rest and quiet. For more than thirty years, the Chief had paid his periodic visits to his white friend, at whose wigwam he could have fresh air, good food and restful home comforts. When the doctor suggested that he be taken to the hospital, he protested. He wished to go to the Wigwam and be amongst friends who knew and understood him. He said they had put Iron Tail, his friend, in a hospital a dozen years ago, and Iron Tail had gone to the Sand Hills.

In the foothills of the Alleghenies, trapping grounds of New France's hired Indians in the long ago, the Wigwam had for many years been the meeting place for many of his tribe now gone. Here he had met with Buffalo Bill, Captain Jack, Bob Strahorn, old-time scouts. Here had come, from time to time, Chiefs Good Face,

Lone Bear, American Horse, Plenty Coups, Iron Tail and others. Here were many of the personal mementoes of Sitting Bull, Red Cloud, Wanata, Rain-in-the-Face, Hollow Horn, Crow Dog, Iron Cloud, Little Shell, Crazy Horse, and other friends and acquaintances long gone to the Happy Hunting Grounds. Here he himself and his close friend Iron Tail had held a reception once in the long ago, for hundreds of their friends, when bankers, preachers, teachers, business men, farmers, came from near and far along with their ladies, to pay their respects and say, How Cola! He would go to the Wigwam, he said. Jimmy Pulliam had come along to assure care and attention on the trains, and to act as interpreter. On his visit the previous year, Thunderbull had attended him as guardian and interpreter to help in recording his story of the Custer fight. This time, the Chief said he wanted to talk about making over the white man's history, so that the young people would know the truth; the white man's books about it did not tell the truth, he said.

M. I. McCreight

The Wigwam
DuBois, Pennsylvania
November 2, 1946

FIREWATER
and
FORKED TONGUES

Chief Flying Hawk at 62
*and reproduction of his thumb-print used
in signing statements made to the author*

Chapter

1

Flying Hawk

The Chief said he would soon go to the long sleep; he wanted to tell the Indian's side of things that white people had not told the truth about; old-time Indians had no books and could not read; the young people had learned to read and should know the truth about history, he said. On former visits he had related the red man's view of incidents wholly contrary to the white man's historic record of them. These he now wished to review and to add others, and to have them put in book form; Indians tell the truth; white men's paper-talk speaks with a forked tongue, he said.

In speaking of his own life history Flying Hawk said:

"I was born four miles below where Rapid City now is, in 1852, about full moon in March.

"My father was Black Fox and my mother's name was Iron Cedarwoman.

"My father was a Chief. In a fight with the Crows he was shot below the right eye with an arrow; it was so deep that it could not be pulled out, but had to be pushed through to the ear.

"My tribe was the Ogallala clan. Our family roamed on hunts for game and enemies all about through the country and to Canada. My father died when he was eighty years old. He had two wives and they were sisters. My mother was the youngest and had five children. The other wife had eight children, making thirteen in all. Kicking Bear was my full brother, and Chief Black Fox was my half brother and was named for our father.

"When ten years old I was in my first battle on the Tongue River — Montana now. It was an overland train of covered wagons who had soldiers with them. The way it was started, the soldiers fired on the Indians, our tribe, only a few of us. We went to our friends and told them we had been fired on by the soldiers, and they surrounded the train and we had a fight with them. I do not know how many we killed of the soldiers, but they killed four of us.

"After that we had a good many battles, but I did not take any scalps for a good while. I cannot tell how many I killed when a young man.

"When I was twenty years old we went to the Crows and stole a lot of horses. The Crows discovered us and followed us all night. When daylight came we saw them behind us. I was the leader. We turned back to fight the Crows. I killed one and took his scalp and a field glass and a Crow necklace from him. We chased the others back a long way and then caught up with our own men again and went on. It was a very cold winter. There were twenty of us and each had four horses. We got them home all right and it was a good trip that time. We had a scalp dance when we got back.

"We soon moved camp. One night the Piegans came and killed one of our people. We trailed them in the snow all night. At dawn we came up to them. One Piegan stopped. We surrounded the one. He was a brave man. I started for him. He raised his gun to shoot when I was twenty feet away. I dropped to the ground and his bullet went over me; then I jumped on him and cut him through below the ribs and scalped him. We tied the scalp to a long pole. The women blacked their faces and we had a big dance over it.

"The next day I started out again with some men and we ran into a Crow camp. We got into that camp by moonlight, but we got caught. They started to fire on us. We all ran into a deep gulch. We got out, but when it was day we saw them coming with a herd of horses, going back to the Crow camp. We got in front of them and hid in a hollow. When I looked out I saw they had Sioux horses which they had stolen from our camp.

"A big Crow was ahead and the others were riding behind. I took a good aim at the big Crow and shot him in the chest. The rest of them left the horses and ran away. The big Crow was still living. I took another shot at him, then took his scalp. We took all the horses they had stolen. There were sixty-nine head that time.

"Some time after we went to hunt buffalo. All the men went to this hunt. While we were butchering the kill some Piegans were coming. We went to meet them and had a fight. Some missed their horses and were running on foot. I was on a good fast horse. I ran over one and knocked him down and fell on him and scalped him alive (ugh). Another one of my people was close by and he shot the one I scalped. This fight was below where Fort Peck is.

"More Piegans came. More of them than us. We were attacked by the Piegans. I kneeled down beside a sage bush. A Piegan shot at me but missed. I shot at him and hit his horse. It went down. Then I turned back and ran into a Piegan. Four of them were butchering buffaloes. I shot at them but missed. The Piegans ran and left their horses, and I took them all. We killed three of the Piegans. They shot one of our horses through the head. The fight was over and the Piegans went to a hill.

"On the way back we ran into a lot of Crows and we had a fight on horseback. We chased them but no one was killed. We had a scalp dance on the Piegans.

"The next fight I remember was when seven of us went on a hunt of the enemy. We met Crows. The Crows killed one of our men, and we chased them a long way but got none of them. We got back.

"Twenty-two of us went out to the head of the

Yellowstone on foot on hunt of the enemy. The Crows saw us first. They came onto us all at once, yelling, and shooting as fast as they could. They killed one Lakota; they had firearms then. Kicking Bear started after them and I went with him. I took good aim and shot one of their horses. The Crows made a charge on us. We took hiding in the rocks. One boy of our band thirteen years old was shot in the elbow, and one was shot in the back and killed. Another one of our band was shot in the breast but got well. They kept crowding us fast but we kept in the rocks. We made a big yell and started for the Crows. They left their blankets, but we failed to get any of the Crows this time. They had horses but we were on foot, but we got all their blankets and supplies. The Crows quit and we buried the boy on the hill among the rocks. We took the wounded man along.

"Next morning we went into a hill to see if any of the enemy was around. We had field glasses then. We saw a band of the Crows killing buffaloes. All had packed up but one. The one not ready yet I took a shot at but missed him. He ran to his horse and jumped on him. The horse was tied to a stake and when he tried to run away the horse fell back from the tied rope and he fell off. We followed him on foot. He was crying. I shot him and he fell. We ran to him. He had a gun ready and before we could scalp him he shot at one of our men and hit him about the knee. I wounded him but he got up and ran. My brother Kicking Bear shot at him and he fell in a hole. He kept shooting at us. Just then a band of Piegans came after us while we were shooting and we had a battle there. Then a big storm came. It got dark and we got away. We got home all right.

"Soon after that I took a band of seven on foot and we went to look for a fight with the Crows. We ran into a big bunch of Crows just below where we fought Custer. We lay until dark. Then we got into the Big Horn among the timber. We marched single file and stopped along among the trees. I was ahead. I whistled like a whippoorwill. This way we got into the camp of the Crows without raising them. They always kept their horses close to the lodge. We got a bunch of horses and got them away from the camp. I held five of our men to bring the horses. I got a white horse. It had a sheet used for rain. I spread it over myself and the horse. The horse was white too, and so I went back into the Crow camp. I hooted like an owl so the Crows did not know I got back into camp again. I got some more ponies but could get only two of them across the river. I had to swim them over. The other five who had the first lot of horses got them home. We did not see them until we got back and met them at home. That time we got thirty-nine horses.

"On another trip I took twenty-three of my men on foot and went north of Custer field to Bear

Buttes — a long way. We camped twenty times. Every morning we went to the highest hill to look for our enemies. On top of a mountain we saw a camp of Piegans. Then we felt something bad would happen. We stuck needles into our arms and cut a slit in them to learn if we would have good luck in a battle. This we did that morning. After that we waited until dark, then we went down to the camp. They were not expecting an enemy and they had their horses all loose. We got among them and whistled like a whippoorwill to keep them quiet. This time we got a lot. There was one Sioux boy that Kicking Bear got a horse for. We traveled all night with the horses. Next morning when it was light we stopped and counted them. We had a hundred and thirty-nine for this trip. We had to travel at night to keep safe.

"In the winter soon after that we started out again. We camped nine times. We traveled from early in the morning till late and some days we made thirty miles. Then we got another way and slept without fire. A blizzard came. We could not see and we ran into a camp of Blackfeet Indians. We got three horses, each one, and started right back in the storm. Our tracks were filled with the snow. We got in a creek bed and ran into another camp before we saw them. A woman came out and saw us. She told the camp and they fired on us. The horse I was on was hit. He bucked but I stuck to him and we got home. When we were near home I met my brother Kicking Bear, who was going out on the war-path. I turned around and went along again with him and the third one took the horses on home.

"The party of Kicking Bear was thirty-eight, and three turned back. They were going far northwest on the Cannon Ball River. We camped seven times and came to a band of Blackfeet Indians in camp. The Blackfeet are brave and have good nerves. They sneak into Sioux camps and steal our children and take them home and make Chiefs of them.

"We waited till it got dark and got close to their camp. One of the Blackfeet coming out alone ran into the Sioux and became scared. He made a fright-noise, like a wolf scared. We moved back into a hollow place where we could fight. When it was near day we tried to get a bunch of ponies but we could not get away with them. A Blackfoot came out on horseback onto a hill. We took a shot at him but missed him and hit the horse. I saw the horse fall and ran to him. There was a high bank there and the Blackfoot rolled down it. It was about thirty feet. I stopped at the edge and shot at him but missed him. He shot at me and missed. He got away and I went back into the ravine where the other men were, and the Blackfeet surrounded us. We had a battle there. One of our men got shot in the hip but not killed. We finally ran them off.

"When the great Sioux war came we had lots

of battles with the soldiers. We were fighting all the time with Miles and Crook and white soldiers every place we went.

"Some of the Indian agents were honest — sometimes. Jim McLaughlin's wife was a cousin of my wife. I was not in the fight at Wounded Knee, but was there right after the soldiers shot into our women and children with machine guns and killed so many. The soldiers were wrong. They treated us bad. The army of the white people were afraid of us. They did not like Red Cloud because he talked and told the truth about dishonest agents. They put him in the guardhouse at Fort Robinson and put a stick in his mouth [indicated three inches] and tied his hands so he could not talk when the army officers came to inspect. Sitting Bull was all right but they got afraid of him and killed him. They were afraid of my cousin Crazy Horse, so they killed him. These were the acts of cowards. It was murder. We were starving. We only wanted food.

"Crazy Horse was my cousin and best friend. A soldier ran a bayonet through his back. He was unarmed, and two other men held him by the arms when the white soldier came behind and put his bayonet through his kidney. I got there a few minutes after he was stabbed. When he was dead his father and brothers took him away and buried him. They never told where he is buried and now we do not know.

"Crazy Horse was never with other Indians unless it was in a fight. He was always the first in a fight, and the soldiers could not beat him in a fight. He won every fight with the whites.

"The young brother of Crazy Horse was on a trip where now is Utah, and there he was killed by some white settlers. They were having some trouble with the Indians there. When Crazy Horse learned that his brother was killed he took his wife with him and went away but told no one where he was going. He was gone for a long time. He went to the place where his brother was killed and camped in the woods where he could see the settlement. He stayed there nine days. Every day he would look around and when he saw someone he would shoot him. He killed enough to satisfy and then he came home.

"Crazy Horse was married but had no children. He was much alone. He never told stories and never took a scalp from his enemies when he killed them. He was the bravest Chief we ever had. He was the leader and the first at the front in the Custer fight. He never talked but always acted first. He was my friend and we went in the Custer fight together.

"I was thirty-two years old when I was made Chief. A Chief has to do many things before he is Chief — so many brave deeds, so many scalps and so many horses.

"Many times I went out to a hill and stayed

three days and three nights and did not eat or drink — only just think about the best way to do things for my people.

"When about twenty-six years old I was married. I got two wives. They were sisters. White Day was the name of one, and Goes-Out-Looking was the name of the other one. They belonged to the same tribe, but now they are both dead. Only one child. His mother was Goes-Out-Looking and his name Felix. White Day had no child. My years now seventy-six, and soon I will be along with Iron Tail and Red Cloud.

"When my father was dead a long time we went to see how he was on the scaffold where we put him. His bones were all that was left. The arrow-point was sticking in the back of his skull. It was rusted. We took it home with us.

"When my brother Kicking Bear died he was put in a grave on a hill. All his things were put in the grave with him. I will see his son, Kicking Bear, if they will let us dig open the grave and take out the arrow-head and send it to this wigwam to put along with my things."

It was late when the old Chief completed the telling of the story as above recorded. He signified a desire for a smoke and the Red Cloud peace-pipe with its long ornamented stem was brought from the cabinet, and some red-willow bark mixed with tobacco for the old-time kinnikinnick, which the Chief enjoyed, as between puffs he recalled notable Councils of Treaty with Government agents. He said they always talked with "forked tongues" and did not do as they agreed on in the paper.

Chapter
2

Early Episodes of United States History

Comfortable chairs, a table and writing materials had been placed in the sun-porch adjacent to the library, and the old man began by telling how Columbus was well treated by the natives, but when he left for Spain, he forced several of them aboard his ship along with him and sold them as slaves, leaving them there to die with homesickness and despair; that other ships captured and took great numbers back and sold them into slavery, and that when they tried to colonize the islands, they forced the natives to work so hard that the whole race was exterminated.

Jimmy Pulliam asked the Chief to say something about Montezuma, but all he said was that the Spanish captain was a ruffian called Cortez, who went amongst the natives with guns and horses, stole their gold and killed them same as wild animals, destroyed their books and houses because they had a different God. Sica! (all bad) — the Chief said, and asked for a drink of good wine. This was brought him, and he signed that he was tired and would like to sleep. He refused to be sent to a

bedroom, and asked to have the buffalo robes and blankets; with them he made his couch on the open veranda
floor, where he retired in the moonlight, and rose with
the morning sun for a breakfast of bacon and eggs, with
fruit and coffee.

After a walk through the nearby woods, the Chief
loaded his redstone pipe and smoked it while seemingly
collecting his thoughts for another talk. He said after
Cortez and his fanatics had annihilated the Montezuma
rule and destroyed a civilization in many respects superior to their own, a governor of a district of Panuco brutally carried away and sold ten thousand natives as slaves;
chiefs were tortured and burned when unable to furnish
more gold; whole towns were depopulated and
destroyed, and the country made a desert.

When Coronado went in search of stores of gold
reported to be in possession of natives far to the north,
he plundered the villages of the Navajos and allied
tribes in the Arizona and New Mexico country; those not
deliberately slaughtered were put in slavery. Under this
bondage, the natives suffered for forty years, then turned
on their brutal taskmasters and killed four hundred of
them, and for a little time recovered freedom. But soon
a larger army came from the Cortez country, when the
home of the oldest of all natives was again brought under
Spanish control for three centuries. It was not a very
good beginning if the white man wanted to make Christians out of them when they knew as much about God as
the Spaniards did, the old man said.

Prompted by his host and Jimmy Pulliam, the Chief

talked about Raleigh's expedition of 1585. He said the Englishmen were treated well by the natives, who gave them tobacco, corn and tomatoes, and showed them how to cultivate and use them, and that the white men became rich from them. For their kindness extended them by the natives and the great wealth they derived from these presents, they killed several natives for taking a tin cup which later was found to have been misplacd by one of their own men, and not stolen at all.

He told of the execution of an Indian Chief for pulling down a piece of tin from a tree to make a pipe for himself. It had been tacked up to claim a section of New Jersey for some royal potentate, by some white men who had come amongst the Indians, lived from their kindnesses in way of food which they lacked. Then because this old Chief had come across the shining tin on which had been scratched the coat-of-arms of a foreign king, and tore it away, they held a trial, convicted the Chief of dishonor and disrespect for royalty, and hung him to the limb of a liveoak tree. When the natives got time to talk it over, they cleaned out the whole gang of white pirates and burned their cabins. Washta! (Good).

Speaking of John Smith's Jamestown settlement, the Chief said that Smith was not honest with Powhatan; compelled him to furnish corn and supplies without paying him for them; took little Pocahontas and held her prisoner so that he could control her father.

Here the old man began a rapid dissertation directed to the interpreter. His Lakota dialect accompanied by sign language was too rapid for the host to comprehend.

When finished, the interpreter outlined what he wished reduced to white man's words: It was to show that the red man was receiving the same kind of misrule and outrageous exploitation that Powhatan had received. The Chief lit his pipe and relaxed while Jimmy related the old man's attempt to enlighten him. He was telling Jimmy of the cheating of the Osages in Oklahoma, and that it had been published by the Indian Commission in a recent annual report. This report the host had, and stepping to the library brought it out for Jimmy to read to the Chief. How! how! the Chief said, and demanded that it be written into his statement.

Following is quoted from the Indian Commission's annual report for 1926:

A situation in which these Indians find themselves, a situation developed by white men without regard to the interests of the Indian — nor can we ignore the unhappy fact that for eighteen years or more, these wards of the United States, living in forty counties of eastern Oklahoma, have been shamefully exploited by a group of guardians and their attorneys, whose unconscionable deeds are matters of public record and of common knowledge. The land and money stolen from the Indians cannot be given back to them — but it is not too late for Federal and State authorities, legislative and executive, to adopt measures to prevent further evil exploitation of these Indians, and to safeguard their interests and promote their welfare. It is common knowledge that grafting on rich Indians has become almost a recognized profession in Eastern Oklahoma, and a considerable class of unscrupulous individuals find their chief means of livelihood and source of wealth in this grafting; so common is it that the term grafter carried little or no opprobrium in Oklahoma.

Long ago the Indians were forced into Indian Territory, because it was land the white man did not then want. Then oil was found, and the white man wanted it very much indeed, but now they could not force the Indian to leave — they had to pay him for the oil. They gave him money for the oil, then cheated him out of the money, as above noted. A sordid tale with little variation that began with the landing of the Norsemen nearly a thousand years ago!

After a good smoke, his last command was interpreted. It was the Chief's desire to have a glass of wine and the lights turned out so that he could sleep. He would talk again tomorrow.

Rain having come on, the robes and blankets were transferred to the sun-porch, where he was protected from inclement weather, for, as previously noted, he could not be induced to sleep on a white man mattress and springs.

At sun-up the Chief was missing. Breakfast was delayed. Presently he was seen coming from the forest which nearly surrounds the Wigwam. In his hand he carried a green switch six feet in length. From his traveling bag he took a bundle which he carefully unfolded and laid out — a beautiful eagle-feather streamer which he attached to the pole at either end. After testing it in the breeze he handed it to his friend with gentle admonishment to keep it in a place where it could always be seen. It was the Chief's "wand," and he said it must always be kept where it could be seen, else the people would not know who was Chief. Having disposed of this, to him, important duty, the Chief was ready for breakfast.

Rested and refreshed, the old sage of the Lakotas was disposed to talk about his people and their unfair treatment through the centuries since Columbus came. It was a fine chance to get the viewpoint of the red man on some episodes in American history that have been told by the white men but about which the Indian has not yet been heard.

Asked about how the red men looked upon the story of John Smith and Pocahontas, the Chief proceeded to tell their way of thinking about the romantic tale. He said:

"That Virginia venture was a gold-hunting expedition like when Cortez went to steal from Montezuma the Indians' gold and silver and land. They were a lot of fellows out of a job who wanted to live without work by cheating and robbing the native people who did not have guns.

"Powhatan was kind to them when they came. He gave them food and helped them to make houses to live in. They stayed a long time and did not work and raise food but got it from the Indians. Then when the corn was not plenty for all, Smith told Powhatan that they had been wrecked and soon ships would come from England and take them back home. Ships came and put more English people on the land but did not bring food for them. They were hungry and asked for more corn from the Indians, but there was not enough for all, and so Powhatan told them he had food only for his own people. The white men had guns and swords and told Powhatan he must give them the corn or they would kill his people. Then there was trouble. They took the food from the Indians and the Indians killed some of them and then they became enemies.

"It was when they had stolen a lot of food from the Indians and were in camp to eat it that Smith said Pocahontas came to them through the path in the woods and told them the Indians were coming to kill them, and she put her arms around Smith's neck and cried. It was a good white man's story, but Indians do not believe it as it is not their way of killing white men. Smith did not tell this story until long after he went back to England to put it in his book. Pocahontas was a girl only twelve or thirteen years old and Smith was a hard man more than forty or fifty winters. Rolf took her to England but she did not live very long there so far away from her people.

"It was the same with John Smith as it was when Columbus got among the Indians. They liked them and were friendly as long as the natives gave them food, and then they tried to take everything they had from them and make slaves of them to do their work. The Indians did not have the same kind of God and so they did not treat them like men but like animals. Columbus made the Indians dig in the mines for gold, and if they did not find it he killed them, until all of them on the island were killed or made slaves for his men."

NEW AMSTERDAM

Referring to the purchase of Manhattan for a lot of fish-hooks and trinkets valued at twenty-four dollars, the Chief's countenance indicated that it was the best kind of argument to prove how the white men cheated the innocent red folks on every occasion. The Indians had befriended the helpless adventurers when they came among them, and for their kindness the settlers attacked them one night and killed more than a hundred and twenty men, women and children while they were asleep in their wigwams. This was about the first massacre. But it was a white man massacre of Indians. They ran their bayonets through the stomachs of little babies and flung them out into the river. They cut off the hands of the men and cut open the women with their swords. They went among them with a torch of fire and burned their homes until no Indians were left; and these all were friendly Indians who sold the white people their island for needles, awls and fish-hooks, and brought the furs to them. (This was in 1642 under Kieft's regime.)

The white man's account of this affair tells us that on February 25th at midnight Kieft sent Sergeant Rodolf with a party of soldiers to Pavonia and another party under Adriensen to Corlear's Hook, where they rushed in upon the sleeping families and killed them all in the most hideous butchery that can be found in American annals.

An eye witness records it in these words:

I remained at the Director's [Kieft] and took a seat in the kitchen near the fire. At midnight I heard loud shrieks and went out on the parapet of the fort to look . . . at the flash of guns. I heard no more of the cries of the Indians; they were butchered in their sleep. Sucklings were torn from their mothers' breasts, butchered before their mothers' eyes and their mangled limbs thrown quivering into the river or the flames. Babes were hacked to pieces while fastened to little boards; others were thrown alive into the river, and when the parents rushed in to save them the soldiers prevented them from landing.

De Vries said of it:

Some came running to us from the country, having their hands cut off; some lost both arms and legs, some were supporting their entrails with their hands, and mangled in other horrid ways, too horrible to be conceived.

The white man's own history refers to this massacre in the following language:

This crime has hardly a parallel in the annals of savage atrocities, directed as it was, upon a friendly village of harmless, unsuspecting Indians.

But this was merely the beginning of a series of white-man massacres that continued for nearly three centuries.

Chapter

3

Indian Philosophy

ANCESTRY

Asked if he had any definite idea where the Indians came from, Flying Hawk said that the Indians were as old a nation of people as the Egyptians and were here and in South America before the pyramids were built, and they had as good government as any nations in Europe. He referred to the great roads and irrigation systems of the Peruvians and Mexicans; and he called attention to their arts and sciences; their courts and administrative systems; their wonderful architecture, money, and religious establishments.

Asked if the Sioux had any legend about where they came from to settle in the prairie country of the buffalo in the time before they had horses, the Chief said the Sioux people in long ago lived at the seaside (he indicated the shores of Lakes Michigan and Superior), as they had fresh fish and much wild rice and ducks and geese. The stories handed down by the old men told of living in bark cabins before they had buffalo skins for teepees, and they planted squash, corn and beans. He said the French "blackcoats" were the first men they ever knew of with white faces and who wore cloth for clothing, and carried a cross and wore beads and had books with them, but this was in later time after they had horses.

In reply to who the mound builders were, he said they were ancestors of the present-day Indians, and the mounds were built by them just as Egyptians built pyramids to bury their dead in and to show their worship to the Great Spirit. Before Columbus came there were many more people in the country than ever afterwards. The Indian knows how the first man and first woman came about, as well as the white man knows.

"Does the white man know?" he asked. "Who is right if the Indian says his great grandfather was a bear, and the white man says his great grandfather was a monkey?"

"The Great Spirit made yellow people and brown people and black people and red people. Then a few white people came from the north where it is cold; how could they be from monkeys that live only in the hot places? They don't know where they came from but the yellows and browns and blacks and reds were here a long time first and they are many more than the whites, and will be here when the whites are all gone again," the Chief contended.

"The whites have got rich from controlling the colored people of the world but they went too fast and got into debt to each other, and now they fight among themselves. Soon they will destroy themselves and the original races will go on in the way the Great Spirit made them to do."

FIRE AND SMOKE

"White people do not know how to handle fire. They make big fire and smoke and get little heat; Indians make little fire and get plenty heat. Their pipe is high bowl with little hole for tobacco, and a long stem. Little fire, little heat, smoke always cool when it get to end of mouthpiece."

"Indians always carried flint and dry wood to make fire."

While making the foregoing comments, the Chief was engaged in taking down his long hair-plaits, in which were woven strips of otter fur. From his kit sack he took his comb and bottle of bear's oil and carefully combed and oiled his hair, made up new plaits, then applied a little paint to his cheeks, looked into his small hand-mirror, and was ready to answer questions. His hair, now still reaching to his waist, was streaked with grey, and in reply to how Indians were able to retain their hair in such perfect condition, he said they did not always retain it — sometimes they got scalped — but they prided themselves in caring for their bodies. He said that long ago Indians often had hair that reached to the ground. He said that a few years ago he had paid a visit to a band of Sioux at Wood Mountain Lake, Canada, where they lived in the old-time way and had hair that reached to their knees. They were now five hundred, all from seven families who left after the Custer fight when the soldiers came to put them on reservations.

Lighting his small redstone pipe the Chief was asked why the Indians use peculiar shaped pipes and what smoking meant to them and when they discovered the practice. He said smoking was so old with them that no one knows how far back it began. The whites got their knowledge of tobacco from the natives at Roanoke when they came for Raleigh in 1585. The natives called it uppowoc, and showed the white men how to plant it and prepare it for smoking; they took it back to England and soon they used it as good medicine there.

The Indians of the east made pipes of clay, and some carved pipes out of stone of every kind; some of sandstone; some of slate, and some of soapstone. But the western tribes had a place at the head of the Red River, now in Minnesota, where they got a red stone from which all their pipes were made. It was a sacred quarry where once a great battle was fought in which there was so much blood that it made the material red. After that fight it was a peace ground and no fights could be made there, so all the Indian tribes could come there and get the pipestone they wanted and take it away. Tribes that were enemies met there in peace. No other stone is like it and there is no such place anywhere else in the whole United States. When enemy Indians wished to become friends again, they smoked the big pipe made from this stone, and so it was called a peace pipe and was always kept sacred by the head Chiefs. When the Government men came to make treaty with the tribes it was a peace council and the big pipe was always smoked together, he said.

To learn more about this historic place, reference was made to the report of A. P. Rose of the Minnesota Historical Society, a short excerpt from which says:

Without taking into consideration the Indian traditions, it can be stated on authority that the red pipestone, which is found in no other place on earth, has been quarried for several thousand years.

In connection with the pipestone story, and to illustrate that the white man's exploitation of the red race still continues, the Chief turned to the interpreter and in great earnestness succeeded in making him translate to the writer his desire to have incorporated in his talk the claims submitted by the attorneys in the great Sioux lawsuit against the Government instituted in 1923, with regard to swindlings that were perpetrated upon the Sioux tribe in so-called land purchases.

In the Court of Claims of the United States, in the Plaintiff's Paper Book in Case No. D-546, was found a reference to a treaty from which the following statement is recorded on pages 389-390:

The transaction which took place between the United States and said petitioners [Yankton Sioux] in 1858 resulting in the transfer of the Pipestone Quarry to petitioners amounted to this: The Guardian Government acquired title from its wards, free of all legal claim on their part, to approximately 11,000,000 acres of land worth $13,750,000, as shown by its own valuation, for a money consideration of $1,650,000. . . . the Government having derived a direct and immediate pecuniary benefit of $12,100,000.

. . . in other words, plain and simple, it took advantage of its wards by trading land worth $64,820, with them, which already *belonged* to them, for land worth, at its own valuation $12,100,000.00.

This, the Chief contended, is only one instance of many where the white man has admitted his ruthless dishonesty in dealing with the Indians in a public capacity; private exploitation and robbery was much worse, he said.

RELIGION

In the very center of grounds once dominated by Red Jacket, whose name and fame Flying Hawk wished to perpetuate, he directed that portions of his most notable speeches be reproduced for his proposed history, and put his thumb-print to what is to follow.

At the close of the War of 1812 attempts were made to Christianize the people of the Six Nations and try to establish the white man's civilization amongst them. To further this end, various missionaries were sent to convert them. To Red Jacket's home came one Cram, to exert his persuasive powers on the great Chief, urging him to call a Council to hear the white man's gospel propounded. The Chief granted the request; a day was spent listening to the harangue of the evangelist. At the close of the meeting, the Chief said his Council would deliberate for a day, and then he would give the reply of his people. A large assemblage was gathered to hear Red Jacket's reply to the blackcoat:

"Friend and Brother, it was the will of the Great Spirit that we should meet together this day. He orders all things; He has taken His garment from before the sun and caused it to shine with brightness upon us; our eyes are opened so that we may see clearly; our ears are unstopped so that we have been able to distinctly hear the words which you have spoken; for all these favors we thank the Great Spirit.

"Brother! This council fire was kindled by you; we have listened with attention to what you have said; you have requested us to speak our minds freely. This gives us great joy, for we now consider that we stand upright before you and can speak what we think; all have heard your voice and all speak to you as one man; our minds are agreed.

"Brother! You say that you want an answer to your talk before you leave this place; it is right that you should have one, as you are a great distance from home and we do not wish to detain you. But we will first look back a little, and tell you what our fathers have told us, and what we have heard from the white people.

"Brother! Listen to what I say: There was a time when our forefathers owned this great island; their seats extended from the rising to the setting of the sun. The Great Spirit had made it for the use of the Indians; He had created the buffalo, the deer, and other animals for food; He made the bear and the deer, and their skins served us for clothing; He had scattered them over the country and had taught us how to take them; He had caused the earth to produce corn for bread; all this He had done for His red children because He loved them. If we had any disputes about hunting grounds, they were generally settled without much bloodshed. But an evil day came upon us; your forefathers crossed the great waters and landed on this island. Their numbers were small. They found friends, not enemies; they told us they had fled from their own country for fear of wicked men, and had come here to enjoy their religion. They asked for a small seat; we took pity on them, granted their request and they sat down amongst us. We gave them corn and meat. They gave us poison in return [whiskey]. The white people had now found our country; tidings were carried back, and more came amongst us; yet we did not fear them; we took them to be friends; they called us brothers. We believed them and gave them a large seat; at length their numbers had greatly increased. They wanted more land. They wanted our country. Our eyes were opened; our minds became uneasy. Wars took place. Indians were hired to fight against Indians, and many of our people were destroyed. They brought strong liquor amongst us. It was strong and powerful and has slain thousands.

"Brother! Our seats were once large and yours were very small. You have now become a great people and we have scarcely a place left to spread our blankets; you have got our country but you are not satisfied. You want to force your religion upon us.

"Brother! Continue to listen. You say that you are sent to instruct us how to worship the Great Spirit agreeably to His mind; and if we do not take hold of the religion which you white people teach we shall be unhappy hereafter. You say that you are right and we are lost; how do you know this to be true?

"We understand that your religion is written in a book; if it was intended for us as well as for you, why has not the Great Spirit given it to us; and not only to us but why did He not give our forefathers the knowledge of that book with the means of understanding it rightly? We only know what you tell us about it; how shall we know when to believe, being so often deceived by the white people?

"Brother! You say that there is but one way to worship and serve the Great Spirit. If there is but one religion why do white people differ so much about it? Why not all agree, as you can all read the book?

"Brother! We do not understand these things. We are told that your religion was given to your forefathers, and has been handed down father to son. We also have a religion which was given to our forefathers, and has been handed down to us, their children. We worship that way; it teaches us to be thankful for all the favors we receive, to love each other, and to be united. We never quarrel about religion.

"Brother! The Great Spirit has made us all. But He has made a great difference between His white and red children; He has given a different complexion and different customs. To you He has given the arts; to these He has not opened our eyes. We know these things to be true. Since He has made so great a difference between us in other things, why may not we conclude that He has given us a different religion, according to our understanding? The Great Spirit does right. He knows what is best for His children and we are satisfied.

"Brother! We do not wish to destroy your religion, or to take it from you. We only want to enjoy our own.

"Brother! You say you have not come to get our land or our money, but to enlighten our minds. I will now tell you that I have been at your meetings and saw you collecting money from the meeting. I cannot tell what this money was intended for, but suppose it was for your minister; and if we conform to yours, perhaps you may want some from us.

"Brother! We are told that you have been preaching to white people in this place. These people are our neighbors; we are acquainted with them. We will wait a little while, and see what effect your preaching has upon them. If we find it does them good and makes them honest and less disposed to cheat Indians, we will then consider again what you have said.

"Brother! You have now heard our answer to your talk, and this is all we have to say at present. As we are going to part, we will come and take you by the hand, and hope the Great Spirit will protect you on your journey, and return you safe to your friends."

Red Jacket told of dining once with President Washington. During the meal, he said, "a man ran off with my knife and fork every now and again, and returned with others; what was that for?" On being informed that there were a great many dishes, and each was cooked in a different manner, and every time a new dish was brought, the knives and forks were changed — and white folks were in the habit of washing the taste away with wine, he said, "Ah, I understand — so general a custom among you must be founded on reason; I regret that I did not understand this when I was in Philadelphia; the moment a man went off with my plate, I would have drunk wine until he brought me another, for though I am fond of eating I am more fond of drinking."

Red Jacket died January 20, 1830, at the age of seventy-eight; his monument is a prominent shaft in the beautiful cemetery in Buffalo, New York. His oratory has been compared to that of Webster, Logan and Lincoln.

After approval of the foregoing quotations from Red Jacket, once more Flying Hawk retired to his buffalo robes and blankets on the veranda.

The next morning, after a breakfast of hot cakes, and maple syrup made in the forest surrounding the Wigwam, a walk among the sugar trees and through the orchard, the Chief drew up his easy chair on the veranda and lit his small redstone pipe for a quiet smoke. He had stripped some clover bloom and was examining it when asked what made it grow.

"The Great Spirit, the Sun, makes all life; without it nothing could live and nothing would grow; no birds, no animals, no people. Indians go to the Happy Hunting Ground when they die; whites do not know where they go when they die."

He said that the white folks had so many different kinds of religion and churches and preachers the Indians could not tell which was good and which was no good, so they hold fast to their own. He said:

"If you want to know what the red man thinks about the white man's religion go and read Red Jacket's talk to the blackcoats. The white people fight among themselves about religion; for this they have killed more than in all other wars; did you ever hear of Indians killing each other about worshipping the Great Spirit? It was for their religion that Cortez and his firegun Spanish soldiers robbed and killed the Aztec people and destroyed a whole nation that had a better government and were more civilized than themselves; if that was a good religion, the Indians don't want it. Before Columbus came a great Indian Chief made a speech to his people when he was ready to die, and this is what he said:

"All things on earth have their term, and in the most joyous career of the vanity and splendor, their strength fails and they sink into dust. All the round world is but a sepulcher; and there is nothing, which lives on its surface, that shall not be hidden and entombed beneath it. Rivers, torrents and streams move onward to their destination; not one flows back to its pleasant source—things of yesterday are no more today; and things of today shall cease, perhaps on the morrow. The cemetery is full of loathsome dust of bodies once quickened by living souls, who occupied thrones, presided over assemblies, marshalled armies, subdued provinces, arrogated to themselves worship, were puffed up with vainglorious pomp and power and empire. The great, the wise, the valiant, the beautiful—alas! where are they now?

"They are mingled with the clod; and that which has befallen them will happen to us, and to those that come after us. Yet let us take courage, illustrious nobles and chieftains, true friends and loyal subjects—let us aspire to that heaven, where all is eternal, and corruption cannot come; the horrors of the tomb are but the cradle of the sun."

Comparing religious demonstrations, the Chief spoke of the Indian Sun Dance and the other ceremonial rites devoted to the worship of the Great Spirit, all of which were carried on with great earnestness and order. Then he told of the old-time camp-meetings of the whites where sometimes as many as several thousand gathered and held high carnival for several days during which not only religious fanaticism, but drunkenness and moral excesses, were rampant. The Chief said:

"Did you ever know of Indians hanging women as witches? . . . Did you ever hear of Indians burning their neighbors alive because they would not worship a God they did not believe in when priest and parson could not agree? . . . But you do know that the whites murdered Sitting Bull because he was holding religious ceremonies with the ghost dancers — the same religion that the white man's priest had taught them to follow!"

"If you will read the journals you will see that for a long time William Penn and his Council held court for the trial of witches, thieves and counter-feiters; for drunkenness, cheating, abuse of slaves and all kinds of evil behavior amongst the whites. Did you ever know of such things amongst the Indians? Indians fought for their rights against other tribes and nations, but not amongst themselves, like the white man always does, and always did! That is because the whites have many kinds of religion; no two of them alike; the Indian believes only in one Great Spirit!"

Flying Hawk could view grounds that once felt the moccasin tread of Conemaugh, Bald Eagle, Logan, Guyasuta, Cornplanter, Red Jacket, Shekellamy and many other renowned leaders of the red race of the long ago — all telling the same sad tale of cruel treatment by the white invaders.

He said it was bribery and rum and their usual demoralizing influences constantly used upon the Indians by the British and American armies during the Revolution, that brought about the killing of Jane McCrea.

"Left to themselves the Indians never abused a white woman, even when a prisoner; it was the quarrel over a barrel of liquor, furnished by the whites, that caused the death of this innocent white girl at Saratoga fight ground. The English bribed them to join with them against the Americans; each side promised big things for their help. The poor Indians did not know what to do, and when the Mohawks and Senecas and other neighbors listened to Johnson, Washington sent three big armies into their home country by the lakes and destroyed all their cabins, killed their women and children, cut down all their fruit trees, burned their crops and left everything in ruin."

To celebrate this awful desecration of the Great Spirit's beautiful land and the slaughter of thousands of his innocent people, the Congress passed resolutions thanking the Great Spirit for giving its army the opportunity to carry out such destruction.

"Only the white man would be foolish enough to believe that the Great Spirit would approve such a course. The Indians know better! They know they will be sufferers for such things! The Indians don't believe that Washington would have done such things if he was along with Sullivan."

Of Brant he had only good to say; much was blamed on him to save the face of the English and Johnson, he insisted.

Dwelling on religious matters, the Chief said that the red man's philosophy was sincere in all matters pertaining to religion; it was not so with whites; they teach one kind of way and do another.

"They tell the Indian that it is wrong to kill, to fight, to lie and steal or to drink strong liquor, and then they give him bad liquor and steal from him and lie to him and cheat him all the time.

"They got the Indians to sign away their land for strong drink. If you will look at the record you will find what I say is true; all the country of

America was got from the Indians for beads and rum or by cheating them."

Taking from the library shelf the first number of the old Pennsylvania State Archives to learn just how the white men began to acquire Indian lands, we found that the first transaction in the purchase of Indian property showed a deed dated February 8, 1673, signed by Tospuminck and Weinamink, for a tract of land on the Delaware purchased by Edmund Cantwell and Johannes De Haes. The homestead was called Meg-kerk-si-pods, and the consideration for it was:

> One halfe Ankor of Drinke;
> two Match Coates;
> two axes; two barrs of lead;
> four hand fulls of powd'r;
> two knives; some paint.

The deed was witnessed by: Peter Jegou, Anthony Bryand and Fopp Outhout.

On the 22 October, 1675, the land was confirmed to these purchasers by Phillip Carterett, Governor of New Jersey Province, and it was for SEVEN HUNDRED ACRES. No mention is made in the Indian deed of the size of the lot bought from them, but in the Governor's Patent the exact boundary and acreage are set forth fully. No doubt the signatures of the two chiefs were secured *after* the delivery of the "halfe ankor" of rum.

The next real estate deal was with Osawath for which the Hendrickson Bros. got a large tract in June,

1675, at Upland, and the consideration was "Two halfe anckers" of strong liquor and hoes, knives, etc.

Seeming to be meditating as he watched the automobiles rush by on the trunk line below the Wigwam, Flying Hawk turned to say that white man's fire-wagons kill more people every year than all the Indians killed in a hundred years.

"The white people will soon be gone; they go so fast that they do not take time to live, but they will learn maybe before they all die. Now they are taking lesson from the Indian; they make their wigwam on wheels and go on the trail like the red people do; Indians make travois and pony pull their teepee; white man's gas car pull his teepee where he wants to go; soon they learn Indian's way the best way; no good stay in one place all the time."

Chapter

4

White Man's Perfidy

With a half grin and chuckle Flying Hawk pointed down at the greensward which formed the border of the veranda amongst the spruce and roses and reminded the host of a grand reception which had been given to himself and Chief Iron Tail fifteen years before, when Iron Tail, after he had shaken hands with the assembled guests, gathered the big buffalo hide about his shoulders, waved aside the crowd and walked away. He spread the woolly robe on the grass, sat down upon it and lit his pipe, as if to say, "I've done my social duty, now I wish to enjoy myself." He had listened to the chatter with little understanding of what was said; he had no common interest in doctors, lawyers, judges and bankers, so why waste his time with them? He was used to receptions—in Europe he had rounds of them from royalty; and in America had been entertained by most of the dignitaries of the country.

The historian Chief reminded that when dinner was served, Iron Tail asked to have his own and Hawk's meals brought to them on the open porch where they ate from the table he now sat beside, while the many white folks occupied the dining-room, where they could discuss Indians without embarrassment. This, he remembered, was a good time, and they talked about it for a long time together, but now, his good friend had left him and was in the Sand Hills.

Then he related a time when he and Iron Tail spent an evening in the Indian room of the Wigwam going over all the items there including pipes, war bonnets, moccasins, and other paraphernalia once belonging to Wanata, Red Cloud, Sitting Bull and other of their old-time friends; and he said that Iron Tail told him it made him sad when he looked at all these things.

The host put the question to learn from the Chief the outcome of the lawsuit which he had called the Council to originate in 1923—the expense to attend which the host had advanced to him—against the United States Government. The old man became interested at once to talk about it.

He stroked his breast to show that he was poorly dressed; he was still wearing a coat and vest which had been given him by the host on a previous visit. He said that if he had what was due him from the Government he could dress like other people, and have plenty to eat all the time; much of the time he was hungry and could not buy medicine or go to the doctor when sick.

As he tried to discuss the case, he had frequently to appeal to the interpreter to assist in making clear all

that he had in mind. He wished to show how the treaty
with Napoleon was broken at the time that his country
was purchased, and that the whites had, from the beginning of relations with their tribe, ignored and wholly
repudiated their first and principal obligation toward
the Sioux. The library was searched to locate a copy
of the Plaintiff's Petition filed May 7, 1923, in the
Court of Claims, No. C-531. Section IV in that statement is quoted from the treaty signed April 30, 1803:

The inhabitants of the ceded territory shall be incorporated in
the Union of the United States, and admitted as soon as possible,
according to the principles of the Federal Constitution, to the enjoyment of all the rights, the advantages, and immunities, of the
United States; and, in the meantime, they shall be maintained
and protected in the free enjoyment of their *liberty, property* and
the *religion* which they profess.

Now, did the Americans carry out that treaty? No,
they did not; they failed in every one of the conditions,
just as they did with every treaty they ever made with
with Indians. They agree to something and do something else, the Chief said.

"My father and my grandfather were inhabitants of that territory; I, and my family, and my
friends have been inhabitants of it; we live in it
now! Have we had the right to enjoy our home?
Have we been maintained and protected in the free
enjoyment of our liberty, and our property, and
our religion?"

The old man had left his chair and was pacing
back and forth across the floor; he was showing his

aroused temper. Suddenly he stopped, faced his host
and the interpreter—still seated at the writing table
three yards back — and began a fifteen-minute oration
in his native (Lakota) dialect, emphasized by expert
sign-language, to prove his points.

It was thrilling; it was earnest, eloquent and con-
vincing; compelling comparison to the best in the white
man's records. It was his review of the fabulous sums
expended by the Government over the past three quarters
of a century in fighting Indians. Reduced to plain
English language and written form, this is what the old
Chief put his thumb-print to in verification of what
he had argued so ably to prove.

Government reports show that from 1776 to 1886
more than nine hundred and twenty-nine million dollars
had been spent in fighting Indians; and in the ten years
from 1872 to 1882 the cost was two hundred and two
million, nine hundred and ninety-four thousand dollars.
He spoke of Mormons taking cattle to Utah in 1852,
when, as they passed Laramie, an Indian killed one of
these cattle. The Mormons complained to the commander
at the fort, who sent an officer and twenty men to demand
surrender of the Sioux who had killed the cow, in default
of which they would be fired upon. The Sioux party
offered to pay for the cow; the offer was refused, the
men were directed to fire, and they obeyed. In twenty
minutes the soldiers were all killed and scalped; it was
the beginning of the Sioux war of 1852, which cost the
Government twenty million dollars. A negro servant

insulted a Navajo Indian, who drew bow and shot the negro, who later died from the wound. The officer demanded delivery of the Indian boy; his tribe refused to give him up; the army marched against the Navajos; three campaigns were made against them and they were beaten each time. These campaigns cost the Government twenty million dollars.

Later some cattle were missed by white herders and they saw fit to blame it on Indians. Troops were sent, without an interpreter, against the Cheyennes and Arapahos to punish them for something of which they were not guilty; the soldiers attempted to take away their bows and arrows by force. This cost the Government many lives and more than a million dollars.

One of the bloodiest was the uprising of 1862; this was when the whites were fighting amongst themselves. A contractor of Indian supplies sent to the Sioux agencies a great stock of labeled "prime" mess pork; instead it was made up of heads of hogs and the Indians refused to accept it. It was unfit for food, but because the Indians could not use it, the soldiers were sent against them and as fast as they were captured by these fifteen thousand troops, they were hung. As many as thirty in one day were thus ruthlessly executed because they refused to be cheated by crooked Government agents.

From 1876 to 1886 the War Department spent for maintaining troops in campaigns against the Indians, two hundred twenty-three million, eight hundred and ninety-one thousand dollars. During 1868 and 1869 the cost for eleven months of campaigns against the Cheyennes and Comanches was one million, fifty-seven thousand, five hundred and fifteen dollars, and the campaign against the Sioux in 1876 cost the Government two million, three hundred and twelve thousand, five hundred and thirty-one dollars, besides two hundred eighty-three soldiers killed and one hundred twenty-five wounded, while the Indians' loss was eighty-five men. The Nez Perce campaign of 1877, lasting three months, cost the Government nine hundred and thirty-one thousand, three hundred and twenty-nine dollars and two hundred forty-one lives. The Indians' loss was one hundred fifty-eight. The Apaches cost the Government one hundred thousand dollars for every one of them that the soldiers ran down and captured.

All these troubles and waste of public money were caused by the infamous injustices of the whites. Fighting, the Chief said, ended with the cowardly massacre of Indian men, women and children by the Government soldiers at Wounded Knee. They were suffering from hunger then, and they suffer from hunger now. They still wait for the justice which was promised them in countless solemn treaties entered into with the Government, all of which were faithfully kept by the Indians but all of which were ruthlessly broken by the Government. Although six years have passed since filing suit for more than three quarters of a billion dollars due from the Government to the tribe of Sioux, the debt is still unpaid; its members suffer from neglect, preventable disease and death, as they wait.

A few hours ride to the south of the Wigwam lies buried, beneath a very ordinary monument, the body of General St. Clair. This the Chief was told, and asked what he thought about St. Clair's disastrous campaign. His reply was:

"He was a poor soldier to fight Indians; he had no good soldiers to help him; they were afraid of the Indians and nearly all got killed before they could reach their fort. They had no right there and they got what they deserved, but next time General Wayne got plenty horses, good guns and lots training and a big army to fight the Indians at the cyclone place. He had more men than the Indians, and he destroyed their corn and burned their wigwams; the Indians had no food and went away. It was all wrong. The whites did not buy the lands there from the Indians; they did not make honest treaty with them; the English did not help as they promised to do. It was the same way the whites always did to the Indians. They got a few of them drunk, then got them to sign a paper that they did not understand and the tribes did not agree to that kind of cheating, and when they refused to keep such a trick as an honest bargain, the Government sent its armies to drive them out."

The Chief said that the Government's Commissioners were sent to make a treaty with the Indians, and that

Wayne was wrong and had no business there. On looking up the record it was found that these Commissioners were Benjamin Lincoln, Beverly Randolph and Timothy Pickering. They had been instructed, in event of need to secure peace, to give back to the Indians the lands wrongfully claimed under spurious treaties about which the Indians so bitterly complained, but Wayne would not hear of such interference with his army plans, and went on with ruthless destruction. Which side was right? Did the Government have two different and conflicting orders out? Commissioners with instructions to treat and make concessions, and an army with orders to disregard treaty and destroy the natives!

This was in the spring of 1793. It was in late fall of 1791 that the Indians had so overwhelmed St. Clair's army there, killing more than six hundred soldiers with little loss to themselves. It was an unjust invasion of their home lands and hunting grounds, and they fought for their rights, and won. Now that the Revolution was over and settlers were flocking into the Indian domain in search of free lands in rich Ohio and Wabash country, the new Government was called upon to compel the red race to relinquish its claim and move on. In plain words, they must "get out of the way or take the consequences" at the hands of the military arm of Government.

On February 25 (1793) President Washington called a conference of heads of departments, State, War and

Treasury, with the Attorney General, at his house, where the Indian troubles in Ohio were discussed:

1. Should the treaty with the Indians proceed?

Yes: 4

2. Has President and Senate power to relinquish?

Yes: 3   No: 1

3. Will it be expedient, for peace?

Yes: 4

On February 26 the Secretary of State (Thomas Jefferson) by way of clearing away confusion regarding his vote against the right of the Government to relinquish title to Indian lands (in Ohio) wrote the following (Jefferson, Vol. I, p. 341):

> I considered our right of preemption of the Indian lands, not as amounting to any dominion, or jurisdiction, or paramount-ship whatever, . . . but of preventing other nations from taking possession, and so defeating our expectancy; that the Indians had the full, undivided and independent sovereignty as long as they choose to keep it, and that might be forever; that as long as we extend our rights by purchase from them, so fast we extend the limits of our society. . . .

No satisfactory treaty was made; none was or could be expected to be made under conditions then existing. Wayne's army prevented it even if other influences favored one, and so his army, after months of drill, and well armed and provisioned, set forth, like Sullivan's on its campaign of extermination and destruction, into the Indian homeland. Seemingly, however, there is no record that Congress passed resolutions thanking God for the privilege of wreaking vengeance upon patriot natives who fought to defend their homes and families, as was the case in the Sullivan campaign.

Chapter
5

Conquest by Slaughter

George Catlin, who went amongst the northwestern tribes in 1832, wrote at that time of them:

Trinkets and whiskey will soon spread their charms amongst them, and the white man's voracity will spread and sweep the prairies. The streams of their wealth to the Rocky Mountains and the Pacific Ocean, leaving the Indians to inhabit and at last to starve upon, a dreary and solitary waste.

Just a half century thereafter this prediction came true and had its climax in the buffalo lands of the Sioux. It had already exterminated the Mandans of the upper Missouri and had made sad havoc with the Crows, Cheyennes and Shoshones of the Wind River and Yellowstone sections.

The last of the buffalo were slaughtered by the voracious hide-hunters in 1882-83 when as many as a quarter million hides were shipped from one station in one season. The prairies were a veritable bone-yard; it was truly a drear and desolate waste. The country of the red man was ruined; his food was gone; he had no longer buffalo skins to make covering for his teepee to protect him from the terrible storms of winter, nor to make the robes to sleep upon, or to clothe himself and family.

One can hardly appreciate the calamity that befell this once free and happy nation, to find, suddenly and without warning, the source of their food, shelter and clothing cut off, and the entire population left to wander about helpless and hopeless victims of "the white man's voracity."

Few white men now living know and understand just what happened or how and why. Most of them did not see, or if they did see, did not care—they were the hide-hunters. Their business was to get all they could and get away.

With all the terrible massacres chargeable to the white men there is none that equals the period of the late seventies and the early eighties when the merciless campaign of starvation was made against all the red folks. The long list of slaughtering of the individual bands was as nothing to the awful wholesale annihilation of the tribes that came with the extermination of the buffalo by the heartless hide-hunters from 1877 to 1884. It was as if all the power of the people of the Government following the Civil War, with all the arms available, with all the ex-soldiers who had fought for four long years amongst themselves, were suddenly turned upon the helpless and unarmed red people to drive them from the earth.

The whites could not fight them fairly and win, and

so they let loose all the forces of war upon their source of food and clothing and thus won the battle of extermination by cutting off their supply and then waited and watched them starve.

More than twenty millions of buffalo were slaughtered and left to lie on the prairie to rot. The white men seemed to go insane on the subject of killing, and for ten years they lived as if it were for that sole purpose. They turned the vast prairie country between the Mississippi and the Rockies into a shambles. They upset the laws of Nature that had ruled for ages. They turned a beautiful land into a desolated wilderness, a cemetery of bleached bones. They made of half a continent that was full of life and energy and happiness, home of one of the greatest nations that ever peopled the earth, a funeral pyre; a blasted empire.

Nowhere in the history of mankind is there to be found a parallel; nothing so cruel, un-American and wholly inhuman. Cortez in Mexico and Pizarro in Peru carried on their wars of extermination in the name of religion; they felt they were justified in wiping out great nations because they did not worship the Spanish God.

But the white man had no justification for his ruthless campaigns against the red race; they were kind to him always when he deserved kindness. The white man had nothing to gain by his deliberate slaughter of the buffalo, and he did not gain by it.

He did not gain by his deliberate mistreatment of the Indian but brought upon himself endless suffering physically, morally and financially. He is facing the greatest lawsuit in history now, for his disregard of honesty in the days gone by. The laws of God are inexorable, and when they were so wilfully violated as was done in the case of Indians and buffalo, man must pay the penalty—for the verdict will be rendered in the Court of Eternal Justice in this case—not before the bar of mere man.

With the winter supplies of 1884 exhausted in early spring the red man looked out upon a barren prospect. There were none of his familiar herds of buffalo for him to renew his supply of food and clothing. He looked in vain for something to eat and for shelter, and clothing for his women and little children. It was not there. The life that was, now was desolation and despair. Hunger came fast. From the robust frame there looked eyes from hollow sockets, and sunken cheeks took the place of well-rounded countenances. Disease followed, and death.

From that time forward the red man languished. From a lively antagonist he became the supplicating lonely forlorn beggar — helpless, homeless and heart-broken. It was the last great massacre of the red men by the whites.

Chapter

6

Cornplanter and Logan

Adjoining the sun-porch at the Wigwam, the open veranda gave Flying Hawk a wide sweep of mountain and valley scenery; the western summit slope of the eastern Continental Divide. For nearly two centuries it was a choice trapping ground, a part of New France from which beaver, mink and other kinds of fur pelts were transported over pack trails to Niagara, thence to Montreal for shipment to Paris. When told that in these mountains there were bears and deer, and that every season thousands of deer were taken by the hunters, who had hundreds of camps scattered all through the region, the old Chief became agitated. He told how the whites had exterminated their buffalo, and killed off their game animals and their wild geese and ducks so that the Indian no longer had any place to hunt; it was all bad.

This was not news to the host; he had seen it all occur as the old Chief said. His was the job of buying and shipping thousands of tons of buffalo bones to the eastern markets following the slaughter of the last herds, by the insatiable hide-hunters; and these from the Chief's own native country. The host could sympathize with him, but could not justify the crime of which he complained—one of many crimes inflicted upon his race.

Across the valley the Chief's attention was called to the old Indian trail which could be seen with the aid of the field glass, a few miles east. It was the portage and pack-path between the waters of the Susquehanna River and the Allegheny River, at the mouth of French Creek, where the old French fort stood, at which Washington stopped on his way to LeBoeuf. Over this old trail the first white settlers came to build log cabin homes on the choice lands mentioned by Washington in his report. That intrusion was objected to by the Seneca tribe and by the Delawares. Two of their prominent Chiefs, Captain Bull of the Delawares, and Chief Conewyando of the Senecas, captured Darius Meade while plowing in a clearing. In an effort to escape, Meade got possession of Bull's knife and killed the Delaware Chief, but in the struggle with Conewyando, the Chief won, only to die of the wounds inflicted by the dead Meade, whose blood-covered body lay at his side, a few hours later. Captain Bull and Darius Meade were buried in the same grave, dug for them where they fell—unlovely intermixture of the blood of different races!

Flying Hawk was interested to discuss early Pennsylvania history. He referred to William Penn as one who wished to see fair play, good faith and honesty extended to the Indians. He said if Penn had been obeyed by his officials and followers there would have been no Indian wars in his state; but when they began to steal Indian land like was done in the Walking Purchases, and cheating them in every trade by getting them drunk, then the Indians retaliated. For half a century they killed white settlers, burned their homes and crops, took their women and children prisoners. They liked the French best then because they did not take their land, but wanted only furs; but the English cut down their forests, killed their game and treated them as they did wild animals, wanting only to drive them back so that they could possess their country.

He said the terrible Wyoming trouble was the fault of the whites; and then he told of the massacre of Indians by the whites at Conestoga camp as a thing that Indians would not have done without better reasons. His host told how Indians had killed his great grand-father in 1794; how an Indian had hidden behind a log on the river bank and shot him through the groin while steering a houseboat on the Kiskiminitas River but a few miles out of view as they talked, and asked the Chief how he would try to explain such a wholly uncalled-for criminal act. Slow to reply, the Chief wanted to ask if this man was a soldier. Told that he had been a captain in the Revolution, the old man said that either the Indian knew the white man, or was drunk when he did the shooting. Investigation after the affair showed that the Indian had been in Pittsburg, and had been drinking that day, but, as the captain shot the Indian, both assailant and victim were dead, and nothing was done or could be done about it.

While talking about old days in Pennsylvania, the Chief asked if this was not the state in which Logan lived. He was told that Logan's old home was over the mountains toward the east only two hours drive away; that Shekellamy's home was in the same direction farther on, and that Logan was his son. "He was a good friend of the white people; then why did they come in the night and kill some of his family?" There was no explanation; there could be none. He told the interpreter to say that he wished to have Logan's speech put in the book to show that Indians were orators as well as warriors. A copy of that famous address was brought from the library and read to him to learn his reaction to it; when completed by translation, the Chief clapped his hands and said, washta, washta—good, good!

Logan's address was contained in the writings of Thomas Jefferson (Vol. II, p. 88):

I may challenge the orations of Demosthenes and Cicero, and of any more eminent orator, — to produce a single passage, superior to the speech of Logan, a Mingo chief, to Lord Dunmore, then governor of this State. And as testimony of their talents, — I beg leave to introduce it, first stating the incidents necessary to understanding it. In the spring of the year 1774, a robbery was committed by some Indians on certain land — adventurers on the Ohio river. The whites in that quarter, according to their custom, undertook to punish this outrage in a summary way. Captain Michael Cresap, and a certain Daniel Greathouse, leading on these parties, surprised at different times, traveling and hunting parties of the Indians, having their women and children with them, and murdered many. Among these were unfortunately the family of Logan, a chief celebrated in peace and war, and long distinguished as the friend of the whites. This unworthy return provoked his vengeance. He accordingly signalized himself in the war which ensued. In the autumn of the same year a decisive battle was fought at the mouth of the Great Kanhaway, between the collected forces of the Shawanees, Mingoes and Delawares, and a detachment of the Virginia militia. The Indians were defeated and sued for peace. Logan, however, disdained to be seen among the suppliants. But lest the sincerity of a treaty should be disturbed, from which so distinguished a chief absented himself, he sent by a messenger, the following speech, to be delivered to Lord Dunmore:

"I appeal to any man to say, if ever he entered Logan's cabin hungry, and he gave him not meat; if ever he came cold and naked, and he clothed him not. During the course of the last long and bloody war Logan remained idle in his cabin, an advocate for peace. Such was my love for the whites, that my countrymen, as they passed said 'Logan is the friend of white men.' I had even thought to have lived with you, but for the injuries of one man. Colonel Cresap, the last spring, in cold blood, and unprovoked, murdered all the relations of Logan, not sparing my women and children. There runs not a drop of my blood in the veins of any living creature. This called on me for revenge. I have sought it; I have fully glutted my vengeance; for my country I rejoice at the beams of peace. But do not harbor the thought that mine is the joy of fear. Logan never felt fear. He will not turn on his heel to save his life. Who is there to mourn for Logan? — not one."

The Chief was tired; he called for a little sherry. Refreshed, he lit his pipe, smoked leisurely for a while,

then suddenly put this question: he asked why it was
that Indians had lived in the land for hundreds of years
without doing any injury to it, and when the white
people came it took only a hundred years to ruin it.
He said:

"How is it for white men to get it all for no pay,
and now they owe more than it is worth?"

"The white man thinks he is wise; the Indian
thinks he is a fool; he kill all the buffalo and let
them rot on the ground; then he plow up the grass,
puff, the wind blow the ground away; no grass, no
buffalo, no pony, no Indian, all starve. White man
is a fool; Indian fool too for he give the white man
corn, potato, tobacco, tomato — all to make him
rich; all the good the white man has he got from
the Indian; all the bad the Indian has he got from
the white man; both fool."

"When the Indian wants a squaw, he goes to
her father and pays him his price; the white man
takes one without pay to her father, but hires a
preacher to tie her to him; when he is tired of her,
he pays a lawyer to untie the rope so he can catch
another one. Which good, which bad?"

Gazing toward the big game country, the Chief was
told that each year the people of the state paid more
than a million dollars for the right to kill deer; and
many of themselves.

"Ugh, much money for ticket; much money
for bullets, more for things to eat, much more for

the stuff to drink; lots of time waste. Indian kill just to get food, skins to make teepees, and moccasins and robes to keep warm; never kill just for fun."

Mention of the teepee turned the Chief's talk to homes and ways of living. He said:

"The teepee is much better to live in; always clean, warm in winter, cool in summer; easy to move. The white man builds big house, cost much money, like big cage, shut out sun, can never move; always sick. Indians and animals know better how to live than white man; nobody can be in good health if he does not have all the time fresh air, sunshine and good water. If the Great Spirit wanted men to stay in one place he would make the world stand still; but He made it to always change, so birds and animals can move and always have green grass and ripe berries, sunlight to work and play, and night to sleep; summer for flowers to bloom, and winter for them to sleep; always changing; everything for good; nothing for nothing."

"The white man does not obey the Great Spirit; that is why the Indians never could agree with him."

The Chief had once visited some of the survivors of the Seneca tribe in New York state, for whose great Chiefs, Red Jacket and Cornplanter, he had great admiration; and he wished to talk of them. He asked if any of the host's books would give details of their lives; he wished to put something in his book to show his regard for them.

Cornplanter, being the older of the two great Chiefs, was born about 1746. His portrait was painted in 1788 for friends in England, but from a mishap the ship which was to take it sailed without it, and the portrait came into possession of Timothy Matlack, whose life the Chief had once saved. He considered it an excellent likeness, and it has since become the standard for use of historians. Cornplanter was a half-breed, the son of a full-blood Seneca woman and white John O'Bail. As in so many similar cases, his mother raised him. That, the Chief said with a smile, is why he amounted to something. The father, O'Bail, left him with his mother, and made his own home in Albany, and there is no record that he ever came back to the Genesee to visit them.

Kion-twogky, by which name he was known in youth, grew up in the district drained by the Genesee River. Telling of his boyhood days, the Great Chief once said: "I played with the butterfly, grasshopper and the frog." When old enough to marry, he took a squaw, and in trying to find a place in which they could live, he found it difficult, for he explained his failure to do so in a letter to the governor in which he said: "I had no kettle or gun." Once his mother told him that his father lived in the capitol, and he went the long journey to see him at Albany; found that he talked in English and the reception was neither flattering nor the visit interesting to the youth. On returning home, he told his mother: "When I started home he gave me no food to eat on the way; he gave me no kettle or gun."

After he had become Chief, by various deals he was granted considerable land on the Allegheny River in Pennsylvania. In a letter to the Pennsylvania Assembly, he wrote:

"The cause of the Indians being led into sin at that time [revolution] was that many of them were in the practice of drinking and getting intoxicated—the English requested us to join—and promised us land and liquor—then after the war was over Gen'l Putnam told me there was to be a council at Stanwix and I was sent to represent the Six Nations—the three commissioners told me the cause of the war [revolution] was heavy taxes and a difficulty about some tea—that they now had established themselves on independence and obtained some land to live on. I spoke and told them I wanted some land for the Indians to live on—they wanted me to use my power to pacify the Indians; I told them I would take my pay in land and they agreed; Governor Mifflin gave me the land."

At a later time he wrote:

"The treaty had been broken by the whites — they tell us the woods are theirs — that they obtained them from the governor — they destroy all the wolves; they get credit from the Indians and not pay honestly according to agreement. When I plant melons and vines in my field they take them as their own; they take our pine trees from us; they bring whiskey to our reservation and get the Indians drunk. The white people who live at Warren called on me to pay taxes for my land and I objected; then they brought four guns with them and seized our cattle; then the militia was ordered to enforce the collection of taxes. To save further trouble, I went to Warren and gave my note for taxes, forty-three dollars and ninety cents. It is my desire that the governor will exempt me for this tax as I am very poor. I desire that the governor send persons authorized to attend to this the fore part of next summer about the time the grass is grown big enough for pasture."

At the Stanwix treaty (1784) Cornplanter consented to cession of a large territory, and at Fort Harmar in 1789 he took the lead in conveying a great area of land to the Government. This incensed his people so much, his life was threatened; after long controversy he gave way to Red Jacket, who became their leader. As always was the case, the whites soon lost their sense of gratitude for the many big things Cornplanter had done for them. In his declining years, he applied to the Federal Government, saying:

"Where is the land — our children and their children after them, are to lie down? — the Americans claim all the land on one side of the lakes, and the English all on the other side, now where is our land?"

For reply, Washington wrote,

"The merits of Cornplanter and his friendship for the United States are well known to me and shall not be forgotten; as a mark of esteem, I have directed the Secretary of War to make him a present of two hundred and fifty dollars, either in goods or money as the Cornplanter shall like best."

A grateful nation indeed! After glittering promises for his influence, and securing it, along with a deed for the whole of northwestern Pennsylvania, it condescended to make him a "present" of two hundred fifty dollars in cash or in trade. It may be safely assumed that he was induced to take it in trade at fifty per cent profit to the Government, the Chief said.

Chapter
7

Osceola

Osceola had been discussed on previous visits and many notes made of Flying Hawk's talks about him. Always the Chief had shown a deep interest in Indians of the south from the traditions handed down through the old men of his own and neighbor tribes. He had traveled in the south. He had become acquainted with the home grounds of Osceola, the Great Chief of the Seminoles; with his dungeon in old Fort Marion at St. Augustine where the brave fighter had been imprisoned after being induced to surrender under a flag of truce—another incident of the white man's broken faith.

He was bitter in his denunciation of the Government's treatment of these natives who were innocent victims of misrepresentation by the slave owners in Georgia and the Carolinas. The cotton planters were mainly responsible for the troubles with the native red folks, he said. Brutally mistreating them, the slaves ran away to join the Indian camps in the swamp lands to the south, where, in case of escape from the bloodhounds set on their trails, they found refuge. Cattle thieves and border ruffians stole stock from the planters and drove it to the Indian country. In both cases the innocent natives got the blame.

Appeals were made to the Government, and from 1835 to 1842 the armies harassed these poor people until they were practically exterminated; not, however, until they had given a good account of themselves, and from campaigns which had cost the Government enormous sums for building of forts and the support of garrisons, where the troops died like flies in the hot malarial jungle lands. The site of old Fort King, after a hundred years, could be identified by litter composed mostly of broken rum bottles; and the burying ground of the soldiers who died there, by the markerless graves covered by tangles of briars and weeds, wholly unlike the usual national soldier cemetery — altogether a sorrowful monument to Government incompetency and mismanagement of Indian affairs.

The Chief referred to the long controversy between the whites, the Government and the Cherokees; the constant abuse and suffering to which they were subjected; and how, like the Seminoles, they were forcibly dispossessed of their homes and hunting grounds in Georgia, and driven, like cattle, to a strange and inhospitable land far to the west. He said that if they had listened to Tecumseh and joined his people to rebel against the whites, it would be a different story now. He severely condemned Pushmataha, saying that he was a traitor to his people, like Spotted Tail had proved traitor to the Sioux in later times, and was scalped by Crow Dog for his tribal treachery. The Fort Mimms affair, which the whites make so much of as a hideous massacre, was merely retaliation for abuses the Indians had suffered from the planters and soldiers for a long time, and was no more than the whites would have done to Indians under similar treatment. They had often committed atrocities equally terrible on the men, women and children of the red race, but the red folks had no printing press, no one to write about it and publish it to the world.

But when finally overcome by years of persecution, and by subterfuge and trickery, a treaty was obtained based on a few irresponsible signatures of drunken sub-chiefs, large numbers of the Creeks and Seminoles were driven west of the Mississippi. One of the conditions of the treaty was that when they reached their new home in the wilderness and were attacked by other tribes, they had the *right* to *defend* themselves.

Osceola's name lives, in countless counties, towns, buildings, steamships, throughout his native land; paintings and statuary of his person adorn the galleries; books have been written and poetry penned about him. But one must search the records to learn even the name of the general who violated a flag of truce of the national Government, in order that he might capture him and place him in a prison dungeon to die of a broken heart — was the old Chief's final word about the Seminoles.

Chapter

8

Red Bird — The Winnebago

Turning to the early records Flying Hawk said:

"How would Lewis and Clark have got to the ocean of the West if Indians had not helped them? They had the best of treatment from all the Indians; then Lewis killed a Blackfoot and they became enemies to the whites because there was no good reason to kill the Blackfoot men. It was the same that all the Indian troubles came from; the white man always started trouble."

"It was an Indian woman who showed them the way."

"Now when the whites took away their hunting grounds and killed all their game, the Blackfoot people are left to starve, like the rest of us. Have the white folks forgot what the first white men saw when they went to the Indian country first? If you will read of Bonneville . . . 'To call these people religious would convey but a faint idea of the deep piety and devotion which pervades their whole conduct. Their honesty is immaculate, and their purity of purpose, and their observance of the rites of their religion, are most uniform and remarkable; they are certainly more like a nation of saints than a horde of savages.' They are 'one of the purest hearted people on the face of the earth.' If the white man had been the same, there would not have been any trouble."

But the old Chief was not content with the search for and reading to him of the Bonneville Papers as quoted above. He demanded that a record be made of the ruthless killing of a lot of innocent natives by the trappers on Ogden's River as told in the Bonneville Papers, and after some delay, the following was read to him and proved to be what he had in mind:

"A great number of natives were on the opposite bank; they leveled their rifles and killed twenty-five of them on the spot; the rest fled to a short distance — then turned uttering the most piteous wailings — the poor wretches made no defense — nor was any weapon launched by the Indians. We feel perfectly convinced that the savages had no hostile intentions, but were gathered through motives of curiosity."

The Chief wished to show that, in the first place, the Indian was kindly disposed toward the whites, and that not until the white man committed some act of treachery toward him did the Indian seek his remedy. It must be fully realized that such remedy could not be found as white men found it — at law. There was no law book for the red man; he had no court to appeal to for justice; no lawyer to argue his case. It was merely a matter of eye for eye and tooth for tooth. Injury had to be compensated for by injury; it was tribal law! No depredation was ever committed by the Indians against the whites except as retaliation for injury first done by the whites against the Indians, the Chief declared with emphasis.

So insistent was he to bring out his point that he referred to several instances about which he was well informed, either by experience and observation or authentic tradition, among which was the case of Red Bird the Winnebago. This he knew had been printed in an old-time book, and due search discovered it in a McKenney-Hall publication of 1849, which was reduced to writing in abbreviated form, for the Chief's approval and thumb-print for incorporation herein.

Red Bird the Winnebago died in chains — a victim of the white man's perfidy. Government officials and employees had committed personal violence upon leading men of their allied tribes who lived on the River St. Peters, heaping upon them indignities they could not forgive, and who, after taking council, decided to enforce the Indian's only law — retaliation. Red Bird, though regarded as a friend of the whites, was ordered by his head men to share in proposed redress for the grievances they had suffered. He went forth and returned without reporting the desired result.

We-Kau, a desperate character, was then ordered to go with Red Bird on a second expedition in the search for white man's blood. The two entered the cabin of Gagnier, whose wife and child were also present. When Red Bird entered the door, Gagnier took down his rifle from its rack and cocked it but Red Bird shot first, killing Gagnier instantly. A third Indian who had followed Red Bird came on the scene in time to encounter the wife of Gagnier, who attacked and took his gun from him, after which he and Red Bird left the place. We-Kau remained and scalped the child in bed as his contribution to the ordered revenge.

News of the killing of Gagnier spread and the Government forces at once organized a campaign of extermination.

Red Bird, to save his people from the contemplated butchery, voluntarily gave himself up to the military along with We-Kau, although the child had, in the meantime, recovered. This ceremony is described by Colonel Mc-Kenney:

The military was drawn out in line; the Indians were in groups on their haunches at our left; on the right, a band of music. In front at ten paces, were the murderers, the magnificent Red Bird and the miserable looking We-Kau. All eyes were fixed on the Red Bird; and well they might be, for of all the Indians I ever saw, he is without exception, the most perfect in form, face and gesture. In height he is about six feet, straight, of the most exact symmetry; I never saw a face so ennobling and winning in expression, a compound of grace, dignity, firmness and decision; there was no ornamenting of the hair; his face was painted red, intermixed with green and white . . . there he stood, conscious that according to Indian law, he had done no wrong. All sat, except the speakers, who said: "we were required to bring in the murderers, they had agreed to come voluntarily and we as their friends, came with them, asking kind treatment of our white brothers." Especially, they asked that the brave Red Bird be not put in chains. Having heard this all, Red Bird stood up saying, "I am ready," then advancing a step or two he paused saying, "I do not wish to be put in irons, let me be free. I have given away my life. It is gone — I would not take it back."

General Atkinson then took charge of the prisoners, handing them over to the civil authorities at Prairie du Chien, where they were placed in close confinement and in chains. Like Osceola, a victim of similar treatment, Red Bird died in prison of a broken heart.

Chapter 9

Pontiac

Flying Hawk was getting weary of the prolonged concentration on old history, and indicated that he would retire soon, but before he called for his glass of sherry and the buffalo robes, he reminded of a former visit when he discussed Pontiac's life and times at some length, which at that time was reduced to writing and signed. He now asked if that part of his story might be added to his present discussions as what he wished to say about that period. This was read over to him and he said "washta" — good.

Attached to the Pontiac chapter was his own comment on the intrepid little Colonel Bouquet, which was likewise included by way of completing his picture of that era of United States history.

Pontiac was not a bad Indian. He was a great diplomat and an able general. He was recognized as such by both the French and the English. While he lived at Detroit the garrison at the fort were his neighbors and friends.

The white man's history is profuse in its accounts

of the trickery and fraud constantly played upon the red people by the English in their effort to win them away from their older French associates. Bribes and false promises had temporary effect upon these unsophisticated natives of the forest, and when DuQuesne and Venango, LeBoeuf and Presqu'Isle together with the patriot's own home town of Detroit finally came into possession of the English, the red men found they had lost a faithful ally and gained a doubtful one. They were not long in learning that the French voyageur had been his mainstay in the trade of the upper lake country, now completely interrupted by the English, who, with the French forts in their possession, became severe taskmasters over them. Bribes were left unpaid, old promises forgotten; arrogance took the place of former friendly intercourse and solicitation. Instead of finding new friends who would be helpful to them, these western tribes learned their mistake after they had assisted the English to acquire a stronghold that made a barrier between the east and the west that seemed for a time unbreakable.

Pontiac knew, better than anyone, the consequences of their error; he lived in the very center of the fur trade district and saw and understood it all. Born leader and organizer that he was, he lost no time in making an alliance of all the tribes affected, to prepare for a final war of extermination against the whites who had betrayed them. These English were appropriating their lands and monopolizing their trade and exacting tribute from them that never was suffered before — they would combine all their people and unite again with the French and drive the hated English from their beloved hunting lands forever.

The Delawares and the Shawnees had had bitter experiences with these white invaders since the days of William Penn, and Pontiac, who was Grand Chief of the Ottawas and friendly with the Potawatomi and Ojibways, Wyandotts, Senecas and others of the northwest, issued a call, that here must be made a stand for their home and country. The line of forts occupied by the redcoats must be destroyed now or the red man's lands would all be taken from him and their families enslaved.

The tomahawk was lifted high, the war dance was on and the fire-brand and scalping knife never rested for nine long years in the hills of Western Pennsylvania and New York and Eastern Ohio and the lake country. Presqu'Isle was captured and destroyed; LeBoeuf was attacked and burned; Venango's garrison massacred and the fort burned; and thousands of settlers' homes burned, the crops destroyed and their families killed, tortured or taken prisoner; Fort Pitt was besieged, but after long suspense finally was relieved — and likewise Detroit itself.

It was a reign of terror the like of which was never known before or since; but like all other similar attempts to save their beloved country, the red people could not withstand the power of the white man's money, his organization, his terrible powder and shooting irons — and, worst of all, he could not withstand his firewater. It was the white man's rum and whiskey that won the long battle for supremacy in the North American continent.

When Pontiac aroused his people to unite and pass the Red Man's Declaration of Independence followed by his Revolution, the line of forts taken from the French, or rather abandoned by them, now in the hands of the English, were captured and destroyed. It was war, just as the patriots later began their war for freedom from the same redcoats. The white traders had come amongst them, appropriated their hunting grounds, corrupted their families and, by the use of rum, cheated and robbed them of their furs. They possessed themselves of the Indians' gardens and camping places. Settlers rushed in and filled the open lands and the choice meadow and valley lands everywhere; they destroyed the forests and wild game, leaving the red man no alternative but to become the white man's slave or fight for his native land.

Their whole country was being over-run; the whites were seemingly everywhere and coming so fast and behaving so defiantly toward them, that the red men saw no way out but war. Pontiac was the Patrick Henry of his day and the revolutionary hero thirteen years later uttered the same sentiment toward the same tyrannical Government — for each it was Liberty or Death.

Pontiac's people having taken the warpath, it was for a war to the finish — they destroyed the forts of the white men and captured or killed their garrisons. The English stronghold at Detroit fell to their hands, then Presqu'Isle at the lake, and then LeBoeuf, followed by Venango at the mouth of French Creek.

Fort Pitt was then attacked and besieged, but it was a formidable undertaking to reach this barricaded stronghold when protected by two wide rivers and well armed troops and cannon for defense. Bows and arrows could not contend with musketry and field pieces at that distance, and so attention was directed to Ligonier and Bedford and amongst the settlers along the highroads and pack trails between. Farmers were killed or taken prisoner, their crops destroyed and cabins burned; scalping and torture and stealthy murder went on along the border until it was a dreary waste and desolation.

But this was not one-sided. The British armies fought and killed and burned and destroyed the homes and properties of the red men just as vigorously as did they, and they had a great advantage — they had guns and ammunition. They could kill the red men at a distance, but the red man had to meet his antagonist face to face. It is well to think of this when estimating results of the Indian's conflicts with his white oppressor.

With all the hideous atrocities chargeable to the red man there are none so despicable as that which stands against the white people who are loudest to complain.

The red man fought in the only way he could fight — it was personal encounter for him, and his arms were the knife and the hatchet, the war club and the torch. He had to get close to his victim, and there was mostly need of secrecy and stealth to reach him — and when he did it was a case of kill or be killed. He did not resort to poison gas or the hand-grenade nor did he hide in a trench for protection. The red man was born and bred to bravery; he was taught to fight in the open, and to meet his enemy fairly, and it was this spirit that cost him his country. He could not reach the white man who could shoot him at long range.

But to combat the rapidly winning red men in this long-drawn and difficult campaign, we regretfully must admit the whites resorted to means of which no red man was ever guilty:

From the white man's own recorded history is quoted the following over the signature of General Amherst, head of the armies in America and in charge of the campaigns against the Indians during this strenuous period. In a message to his subordinate in the field, Colonel Bouquet, who was sent against the Indians in Western Pennsylvania, he writes: "Could it not be contrived to send the small-pox among these disaffected tribes of Indians? We must on this occasion use every stratagem in our power to reduce them."

Colonel Bouquet replied: "I will try to inoculate . . . with some blankets that may fall into their hands, and take care not to get the disease myself." The response of the great general to this promised cooperation on the part of the good colonel at the front was: "You will do well to try to inoculate the Indians by means of the blankets, as well as to try every other means to extirpate this execrable race." To show how successful this despicable and unthinkable outrage worked, Gershom Hicks wrote that "at Fort Pitt the small-pox had been raging for some time among the Indians, and that sixty or eighty of the Mingoes and Delawares besides some Shawnees, had died from it."

In the great Pontiac campaigns the one outstanding

English military character was Colonel Henry Bouquet, who more than any other contributed to the turning of the tide in favor of the whites. Indeed, it is a matter of doubt if the French might not have ended in full control of the United States territory of that time had it not been for the clear head and perseverance of that intrepid fighter and commander. Bushy Run was the turning point of the French-English domination of the west Allegheny country, and it was Bouquet who invaded Pontiac's own country and forced the surrender of the horde of white prisoners then in the red Chief's possession. At his own risk and personal solicitation the Virginians came forward with troops for his western campaign, and it was long before he was relieved of the responsibility for their pay.

It was Bouquet who furnished relief for the suffering lot at Fort Bedford, at Ligonier, and Fort Pitt itself would no doubt have surrendered had not Bouquet fought and won the Bushy Run affair and got through to relieve the weary garrison at the junction of the Allegheny and Monongahela. All were on the very verge of despair and a little time would have resulted in their complete demoralization. It was his sane and sensible and firm stand, his good judgment and diplomacy that won against Pontiac, which brought about a permanent adjustment of the terrible conditions then existing.

And now let us see the end of the great Napoleon — how he paid the last debt. In Cahokia the Illinois tribe was having a drinking celebration on the white man's liquor — probably to put them in proper humor for exacting a treaty from them as was usual by the whites in those days. Pontiac was invited, and he drank rather freely while the speeches and songs and whiskey bottle circulated amongst them. When the affair was over he walked "majestically" down the street to the adjacent woods; there he was heard to chant his medicine song in the silence of the trees. An English trader, too cowardly to act on his own volition, bribed a Kaskaskia drunken Indian, for a barrel of whiskey, to murder the great Chief. "A silent form crept behind him, a twig snapped, and as Pontiac turned to see what disturbed his meditation, a tomahawk was buried in his brain. Thus foully and brutally was murdered the mighty sachem of the Ottawas."

They could not conquer him in a fair fight, but with bribery and whiskey they foully murdered him.

Chapter

10

Tecumseh — The General

Like a meteor that illumines the heavens at midnight with startling brilliancy; like Patrick Henry and Paul Revere, who, when black clouds hung low and threatened Colonial disaster, rang loud the war tocsin and gave their people Independence — so came Tecumseh, the shooting star of the western tribes, to call his men to arms and lead them in their fight for life, liberty and the preservation of their homeland from further desecration by the demoralizing white man invasion.

Pontiac had failed, not from lack of men and management, but he could not withstand the white man's firearms and firewater, nor the ruin of his people by the subtle and serpentlike corruption of them by the spread of disease and death.

Born in 1768 a twin brother to Elskwatawa, the Prophet, sons of a famous Shawano Chief who gave up his life at the desperate battle at the Kanawha in the futile effort to defend his home against the hated whites, Tecumseh, like his father, also gave his life for his country for like reason, when attacked by General Harrison's army at the so-called "River" Thames, in Michigan.

Tecumseh was a child when the whites began fighting among themselves. They quarreled with their king across the water and declared themselves free from his domination. It was just what Pontiac had tried to do for his people, and failed to accomplish. It was a long period of turmoil and confusion for the red folks. Between the ones who called themselves Americans and those who still were loyal to their king and were called British, the poor red men had a hard time; to befriend either was sure to bring down upon their heads the sword and hatchet of the other. Bribery and corruption increased to such a degree that Indians lost all confidence in both Americans and English. Grown to manhood, Tecumseh saw the Americans win their war for independence, but in his country it seemed to have no effect. The British still were in control, and for many years the bloody contest continued from the Ohio to the Lakes region, seemingly with both Americans and British arrayed against the red folks.

The British had got the Iroquois tribes to cut away their old friends the French, then when they fought with the Americans and lost, the Americans turned on them and sent Sullivan to destroy their homes and kill their families. In the Ohio country, the Indians tried to do as the Americans wanted. They made farms and raised corn and listened to the blackcoats and became Christians.

Then American soldiers came. They told the Indians

they were going to take them to Fort Pitt where they could have better homes. They got them to give up their guns and come together at the two large cabins. When they had all assembled with their women and children, the soldiers locked the cabins and placed guards around them, then told the poor people to offer prayers as they would all be killed next day.

All night these helpless prisoners prayed to the God that white men had told them was their savior; all night the wails of the women and the cries of the little ones came from behind the barred doors. At break of day, the white brutes entered, and with heavy wooden mallets crushed the skulls of the kneeling, wailing women, as they screamed for mercy, as the horrified fathers and children looked on. When the maul-wielder became exhausted with the slaughter of the first dozen, he gave way to another member of his party, who continued until relieved in like manner by his companion. Thus in turn the entire band of ninety-six innocent and defenseless natives were hideously murdered and the floors of the cabins ran red with blameless blood.

When the natives of the district resented this sort of treatment the Government sent its army against them under St. Clair, who was defeated and driven out, only to be followed by Wayne with a larger and better armed force, resulting in a compromise treaty.

During all these troubles Tecumseh was growing into a competent student of current affairs. He became a great statesman, orator and leader of his people; he was the George Washington of the red race.

Keen student of what had transpired between the British and their Colonials who had won independence, Tecumseh decided it was time for his people to follow the same road. So he organized the red tribes of the west to oppose the further advance of the hated whites into the Illinois, Indiana and Michigan country. Proffered aid by the British, who had disregarded the treaty ending the revolution and refused to surrender the western forts, Tecumseh joined forces with them and was made a General and served with distinction under English army regulations.

The new war of 1812 between the Americans and the British came on. Harrison was governor of the Northwest territory, having won from the French the old fort at Vincennes. There he was strongly reinforced with added troops, and the country of the Wabash and Illinois was rapidly filling with hordes of new settlers, making it constantly harder and more difficult for the natives to resist them. During the absence of Tecumseh while organizing his warriors at the south, Harrison attacked and won a fight at Tippecanoe creek, driving the Indians, under Stone Eater, toward their English backers at Detroit, there to await the outcome of the struggle that was to decide the supremacy of the Americans in October, 1813, at the River Thames where the Indian contingent were entrapped. Tecumseh was shot by Colonel Johnson with his pistol, thus ending the life of one of the greatest Indians who ever lived.

It required a long time and much research to get Tecumseh placed in history to suit the old Chief, for he regarded him as one of America's great men — comparable to the greatest of white men; a man whose military genius was not inferior to Washington or Jackson or Grant. Only his lack of modern arms, and the terrible effect wrought by the white man's whiskey, prevented him winning his war for independence. For his manliness, his ability as an orator and statesman, his integrity and physical valor were unequaled by any white man, the old Chief declared earnestly.

Tecumseh was not killed in battle; the white man was afraid of him and they murdered him just as they got rid of Pontiac, Osceola, Cornplanter, Sitting Bull, Crazy Horse and other great Indian generals, the Chief contended. White men know this — they named one of their best generals for the Chief; and the British Crown granted to his widow a pension for life because they recognized his worth. But do they set up monuments and tell the truth in their history? No.

Chapter

11

Black Hawk

Flying Hawk turned to telling of the treaty of 1830 which took from the Indians all their best land along the Mississippi and made the great states of Indiana and Illinois from it and drove the Sac and Fox and the Potawatomi and Winnebagoes, which they did not kill, to starvation and ruin. He told how they took advantage of Keokuk through graft and presents to get his cooperation, and then by hideous massacres of those who refused to approve his crooked bargains, they took and held by force what they got by trickery and subterfuge and without just compensation.

"If the white man's history was true, it would tell how these treaties were got by making the leaders drunk so they would not understand what they signed. Black Hawk was honest and he represented the people who had been so ruthlessly cheated in the crooked negotiations with Keokuk, and the white politicians could not control him, but sent big armies to exterminate them and when they had nearly all of them killed and the rest driven away, they got Black Hawk a prisoner and sent him to Fort Monroe to a stone cell but soon President Jackson let him out to go and live on the Desmoines River where he died and was buried Indian fashion. The white men were not satisfied when he was dead, but robbed his tomb of his bones to make money out of them — but thanks to the Governor, who learned of this ghoulish outrage, he compelled the thief to return them to his people."

Shortly before his death Black Hawk addressed his tribal remnant in a speech to his captors thus:

"Black Hawk's heart is dead and no longer beats quick in his bosom; he is now a prisoner to the white men; they will do with him as they wish. But he can stand torture and is not afraid of death. He has done nothing for which an Indian has been ashamed; he has fought for his countrymen, the squaws and papooses, against the white man who came year after year to cheat us and take away our land; you know the cause of our making war; it is known to all white men; they ought to be ashamed of it; white men do not scalp the head, but do worse, they poison the heart. Farewell my nation! Black Hawk tried to save you and avenge your wrongs; he drank the blood of some whites; now he has been taken prisoner and can do no more; he is near his end; his sun is setting and he will rise no more. Farewell to Black Hawk!"

The Chief asked to have read to him the treaty of July, 1830, which led to all the troubles with Black Hawk and his people. It has the names of twenty-eight natives of the Sac and Fox nations in addition to the supposed signature of Keokuk himself. Then he said:

"How can any white man believe that a drunk Chief and a dozen other common members of each tribe could sell the rights of two great nations in all the land of three great states? And the Government agents did know that they could not; it was always the same; it was as Black Hawk said: 'they came to cheat us and take away our land' — it was a grand steal."

"Do you want to know why Lincoln did not stay long in the war with Black Hawk? I will tell you; he was honest; he knew that it was not an honest war!"

And the old Chief gave a sweep of the arm, saying, "lila-sica" — very bad! He had talked enough.

Chapter
12

Wanata

While examining personal belongings of Iron Tail hung about the walls in the Indian room of the Wigwam, Flying Hawk noticed a beautiful tobacco-bag of great age. He asked to whom it had belonged. Being informed that it was a present from Wanata, he was deeply concerned about it, how and why it was possessed by his host. Both had known this famous Chief in the long ago, for he had been dead for nearly forty years. He was past ninety-five when he untied his belt, took the pouch from it, laid the long-stemmed redstone pipe across it and handed it to the young man as a memento of early Indian days and a souvenir of the Grand Chief of the Sioux.

From the report of Keating, who visited him at the headwaters of the River St. Peters in 1849, we can see him in his prime:

We have never seen a more dignified person or a more becoming dress; a fine mantle of buffalo-skin of white color decorated with small tufts of owl's feathers and other birds of various hues. He wore a splendid necklace formed of sixty claws of the grizzly bear; his leggings, jacket and moccasins were of white skins profusely ornamented with human hair, the moccasins variegated with plumage of several kinds of birds.

In his hair were nine sticks, neatly cut and smoothed and painted with vermillion. These designated the number of gun-shot wounds he had received, and were secured by a strip of red cloth. Two tresses of plaited hair were allowed to hang forward; his face was tastefully painted with vermillion and in his hand he bore a large fan of eagle-feathers which he frequently used. We have never seen a nobler face or a more impressive character while he stood contemplating a dance performed by the men of his own nation.

Colonel Long of the United States Military visited Wanata about this time and in his report is found this comment:

> He is tall and finely formed; his manners dignified and reserved; he is now about forty-five and commands more influence than any other chief on the continent; his rule is absolute; he has no rival or compeer; his mandates are peremptory and absolute.

When known by Flying Hawk and his host, this great ruler and former autocrat had become a wrinkled and half-starved old man; his teeth worn to the gums and his eyes inflamed with trachoma. He stood erect and his hair, still long, was tinged with grey, and showed a lack of the Indian's usual special care.

Instead of the soft white robes beautifully ornamented in bead or quill-work of former days, he wore a faded calico shirt of the white man's pattern, and a shoddy-material coat, trousers and hat. Flying Hawk said that his acquaintance with Wanata was in the times before they were restricted to the reservations so far apart as Devil's Lake and the Rosebud country.

In frontier days, Wanata was a frequent visitor at the writer's office, where he was always treated kindly. One day he signed that he wished a private interview, when he drew from his blanket a package which he exhibited as something he held more precious than any other treasure. It was carefully wrapped in old newspaper, and after it had been divested of the strings and unrolled to be read, it proved to be the parchment or treaty with Government officials, his own name inscribed as head or Grand Chief. Having thus established his old-day tribal office, he carefully refolded the document, wrapped it in the faded news sheet and returned it to the inner folds of his blanket, then nimbly squatted on the office floor, filled his pipe and enjoyed his usual half-hour smoke.

Chapter

13

Washita and Sand Creek

Resuming his discussions on history, Flying Hawk referred to the Sioux treaties of 1851-52. No sooner was the consideration money due than traders and trappers swarmed with claims which they had trumped up against the Indians, few if any of which were legitimate, and totaling four hundred thousand dollars. When the Indians objected to such outrages, Governor Ramsey told the Chief, Red Iron, that he would "break him" — and locked him in the guardhouse for offering complaint against such injustice and robbery of his people.

Flying Hawk said that from that treaty money, they kept out fifty-five thousand dollars for Hugh Tyler which they said was for *getting* treaties through the *Senate,* and for *securing* the *consent* of the Chiefs. Then he gave another instance of deliberate fraud in which the whites succeeded in withholding twenty-one thousand, five hundred dollars "for goods stolen and for horses stolen" which was not true. And then he told of the 1858 treaty by which the Government agreed to pay the Sioux one hundred sixty-six thousand dollars, and never paid it;

but four years afterwards they delivered to them fifteen thousand dollars, in goods, and deducted that from what was due them on another treaty — so that they never got anything for that land at all. (This is verified in Helen Hunt Jackson's *Century of Dishonor,* page 392.)

When the Indians rebelled against this sort of spoliation they might always expect the soldiers to be sent against them, and were seldom disappointed.

Flying Hawk then proposed to tell of the Minnesota outbreak, the Crow Creek affair and other outrages, such as Sand Creek, Baker and Washita massacres of Indians by the United States armies.

WASHITA

"Some of our people stole some cattle when the whites drove away all the buffalo where they were building the railroad, and then they went away south in Washita country where they could hunt buffalo. It was deep snow and cold in winter; they camped in a little valley beside the river; they were asleep in their teepees; they did not know any soldiers were coming. But Custer and his army was following them and came up in the night and found their camp; they surrounded the camp and every soldier had his carbine ready. Custer gave orders to wait for him to shoot his pistol, then all to open fire just before it was light and the Indians got awake. When all was ready and all waited on Custer to fire his pistol, a little papoose began to cry in one of the teepees and its mother crooned to make it quiet. Custer waited till the child was quiet and no noise was in the camp, then he pulled the trigger for signal for all to fire.

"Then the soldiers began shooting into the tee-pees where the women and children were asleep, and killed more than one hundred. The Indian men came out, that were not killed, and went after the soldiers and killed more than forty of them before they could get away; then the soldiers ran off and left their overcoats and a lot of baggage. The white man's history tells that it was a brave battle won by the soldiers; the Indians know that it was a fight of cowards and a disgraceful mas-sacre of innocent natives who were only hunting to get food for their starving families because the whites had come and driven out their buffalo."

After reading about the great battle of Custer, when the sleeping men, women and children met the volleys of United States soldiers at break of day in the winter camp on the Washita, turn to the white author and read the account of Colonel Mackenzie's winter campaign on Crazy Woman's Fork of Powder River in 1876 when Crook's army was taking revenge against all Indians for their victory over Custer.

There were Cheyennes, some of whom had been aid-ing their friends in the fight on Little Big Horn. They were in their home ground and had accumulated ample food stores for the bitter cold of long winter and had gone into their winter camp in a "gloomy gorge in the Big Horn Mountains" where a swift, ice-bound river rushed over the rocks between precipitous walls, which soared into the sky, perhaps a thousand feet on either side. Numberless icy brooks poured their contents into the main stream through lateral canyons, scarcely less forbidding in their appearance than the main one, and which made the trail of the creek almost impossible, and in one of the open places the Cheyennes, under leadership of Dull Knife, had pitched their camp.

Colonel Mackenzie was ordered, with his Indian scouts and ten troops of cavalry, to find and destroy the village. The Cheyennes were not so numerous as the Sioux — but no braver, more magnificent fighters ever lived than this tribe — I believe it will be generally admitted that they were the finest of the Plains Indians.

Mackenzie had seven hundred and fifty cavalrymen and three hundred and fifty Indians . . . halting at the mouth of the canyon, he resolved to await the still hours before break of day — before delivering his attack. The greatest precaution was taken by Mackenzie to prevent his men from making any noise; they stood in ranks by their horses in the snow in that polar cold, waiting for the order to advance — day was beginning to break as they reached the village. The sleeping Indians in the camp had not the slightest suspicion that the enemy was within a hundred miles. The troops, cheering and shouting, burst upon them like a winter storm. Indians when not apprehensive of attack, invariably sleep naked. They had just time to seize rifles and cartridge belts, while the women caught hasty blankets about the children, when the soldiers were upon them. Indeed so quick and sudden was the attack that some of the warriors could not get out of the teepees. With their knives they slashed the wigwams, and from their openings fired upon the soldiers as they galloped through the village. Many were shot dead while a few minutes before they had slept in peace. Most of the pony herd was captured and the village in a short time was in possession of Mackenzie. The Cheyennes, though overwhelmed, were undismayed; they had retreated headlong up the canyon, but were soon rallied by their subchiefs. Dull Knife was found in the village with half a dozen bullets in him — he had fought gallantly in the open until he died. Presently the Indians came swarming back; they occupied points of vantage, and naked though they were in the frigid weather, with the thermometer ranging from ten to twenty degrees below zero during this campaign, they opened fire . . . unless they could be dislodged, Mackenzie's position was untenable. He sent his Indian Scouts to dislodge them — then directed Lt. McKinney's troop to charge . . . was fired upon and killed . . . hit no less than six times; six troopers and a number of horses killed . . . thrown into confusion . . . retreated . . . Hamilton's and Gordon's troops sent to the rescue . . . stubbornly resisted . . . hand-to-hand fighting of the fiercest . . . Davis' troop ordered to join . . . no further reserve . . . cavalry all in . . . would have been wiped out [as Custer was] had it not been for the scouts and Indian hired-contingent; somewhat relieved momentarily, Mackenzie sent word to Crook of his success — and began the destruction of the village. All the winter supplies for over a thousand Indians; the Cheyennes were a forehanded, prosperous tribe; the property destroyed was enormous.

So far, the fight, if it may be called such, was a defeat for the United States troops. If the night surprise and the fleeing of Indian mothers with their innocent babes naked in twenty degrees below zero can be construed as a successful United States army campaign, or a fight conducted in this one-sided and hideous way, a victory to be proud of, then let that part of history be stricken from the record! But the white man's history goes on to say:

Women and children, naked, shivering in the hills, as they saw their belongings consumed by the flames! It was impossible for them to maintain their position during the night; they had to move away or die of the cold; twelve little Indian babies froze to death that awful night. Many of the older men and women were kept alive only by having their hands and feet, and in the case of children, their whole bodies, thrust into the warm bodies of the few ponies not captured by the soldiers, which had been disemboweled for the purpose. The Cheyennes took up a strong position six miles further up the canyon, from which Mackenzie could not dislodge them — and he started on the return trip to camp. Crook, who made a forced march night and day, with Dodge and the infantry — in spite of storm and cold — met Mackenzie retiring just after he left the canyon and the *whole army* returned to the encampment. The subsequent suffering of the Indians was frightful.

It is appalling to think of that night attack in that awful weather upon that sleeping camp — of those wretched women and children, wandering naked in that bitter cold; of the little ones frozen to death; of the old men and women abandoned by the road to die. Yet there is another side to the picture, scarcely less horrible — but why follow the harrowing tale further? It would be but a repetition of what white man's history calls the Sioux War. The white man in his prosperity and boasted civilization tries to forget it; the Indian in his misery, as the principal sufferer, cannot forget.

SAND CREEK

Continuing his account of massacres of Indians by the whites, the old Chief told his side of the Sand Creek affair. He said:

"The Governor of Colorado got all the Indians that were having trouble about whites building roads in their country and driving away all their game, to come to a place on Sand Creek where Fort Lyon was. Here, he told the Indians, they would be protected by the Government troops. The Indians came and brought with them their women and children and made their homes and lived in peace because they could see the flag of the Great Father, and where the governor said they would be safe from all harm.

"Cattle ranch men had some stock stolen and they blamed the Indians, but it was not the Indians. I was a boy then twelve years old. Only a few of our friends were there; the ones at Lyon were some Cheyennes, some Arapahos and some Sioux, and they were all good Indians and did not want trouble.

"Then when they had lived there half a year when it was near winter, the horse soldiers came and killed about all the Indians in the camp; they were soldiers of the governor who got the Indians to come there to live; and some more of United States soldiers were with them; they shot little children, and women they cut open with their swords; they cut off the ears and took their scalps before they were dead; about three hundred they killed and nearly all of them were women and children. Chief Antelope had a paper [certificate] from the army general that he must not be hurt, but the soldiers shot him when he showed them his paper."

An excellent account of this hideous massacre is contained in Helen Hunt Jackson's *Century of Dishonor,* which, with full details of the Congressional Investigation, proves it to have been much worse than the Chief's account of it. Led by Colonel Chivington, a prominent Methodist, the horrifying butchery was given hearty approval by the *Denver News,* and at the theatre the bloody scalps were flaunted before the audience, which "applauded rapturously." However, the Congressional Investigating Committee said:

It is difficult to believe that beings in the form of men, and disgracing the uniform of United States soldiers and officers, could commit or countenance the commission of such acts of cruelty and barbarity.

But, the Chief said, "if the red man's history was in printed volumes, they would contain many accounts of equal barbarity."

Chapter

14

The Baker Massacre

On one of his visits, Flying Hawk had dictated the account of the Baker massacre and signed it with his thumb-print. Now he asked that it be included with his history review.

The period or time does not matter. There is little difference in the records of the treatment of the red men, whether early or in the midst of the rapidly growing civilization.

Malcolm Clark was an agent, rather an employee, of the American Fur Co. in upper Missouri country. One day he beat an Indian boy for some trifling disobedience in the herding of horses, during a fit of his uncontrollable temper, and if there is one thing an Indian cannot tolerate it is an insult of this kind. The Indian's way of getting even for this sort of disgrace is full and complete retaliation. It is his right according to his law and training. The boy exerted his privilege when the chance came. A passing war party heard of the boy's dishonor and joined him for revenge. They killed Clark, as they considered it their right to do; it would have been the same against another red man. Whether red, white, yellow or black, the color of the skin furnished no justification for inflicting injustice — and so the white man paid the penalty.

Fort Shaw was thirty-five miles west of Great Falls, Montana, in command of Colonel Baker. Black Weasel was Chief of a band of Piegans, against whom the Clark affair and some minor depredations were charged, and Colonel Baker was ordered to "round up the Chief and give him a lesson."

Like so many things done by the War Department in the times when it was corrupted with graft and politics through unfaithful Indian agents, post-traders and illicit rum dealers in the far distant posts throughout the frontiers, it acted with the usual lack of common sense and certainly with total lack of wisdom or good judgment.

At this period there was little actual settling of the country so far west; only the traders and trappers and the buffalo hunters and gold seekers were there. Few if any had any legitimate right to be there.

But there was rarely any trouble — certainly none except what was instigated by the miners and rum-peddlers — only trouble that was started by the whites. The killing of Clark was this kind, for if he had kept his place as white men were expected to in the red man's country, there would have been no trouble.

The Piegans and Blackfeet possessed this land; it was their hunting ground, and had been from time immemorial. There were tribal wars with the Crows, the

Sioux and the Assiniboins, who came at times to steal
horses and to fall upon the Blackfeet in retaliation for
some former offense. But from the whites no trouble was
feared or in the least expected.

The Indians were in constant trade with the whites
at the several forts. They traded furs and buffalo robes
for rifles and ammunition and for blankets and whiskey.
Whiskey of the white trader made of the Indians easy
victims for whatever licentiousness he cared to carry on
amongst them. The white man fixed the prices both for
the red man and for himself. Notwithstanding his cheating and constant corruption, the white trader, so long as
he offered no violation of the Indian's sense of justice,
was welcome amongst them.

James Willard Schultz lived amongst them at this
time, and his writings have a charm unequaled by any
other author before or since. He lived their life and he
knew them in the intimacy of the family, in their religion,
on the hunt, in their tribal wars, in sickness and death.
He married a Blackfoot (full-blood) girl, and the story of
the beautiful Nat-ah-ki as the wife of Apikuni has few if
any equals in the romance of the strenuous days of the
frontier.

Bear's Head was Chief of a band of Piegans at peace
with all the world at this time — particularly were they
on good terms with all the whites. They were on their
annual hunt, attending strictly to their own business of
hunting and having a happy time in their winter camp
amongst the trees along the bottom lands bordering the
Marias River in the section marked on the Government

maps as "Lonesome Prairie" about due north from the present city of Great Falls, Montana.

They had been successful in their hunt, they had warm robes for the frigid winter weather, and full supply of dried buffalo meat and choke cherries. They had located for the cold weather in the low ground amongst the trees where the ponies could find grass and protection from the raw winds that swept the higher grounds mercilessly in the long period of zero nights and days, waiting for the signs of spring, when they could be on the move again.

Here they were on the morning of January 22, 1870. Over three hundred of them in eighty teepees — perhaps seventy-five of them full grown men, the remainder being their wives and little ones, averaging the father, his wife and two children to each teepee. There was contentment and happiness here. They had no fear for enemies at this season — perhaps they had no enemies amongst their own race — they had none amongst the whites. And so with wood for fuel and robes for dress and for sleeping between, they defied the blizzards. The women devoted their time to making beautiful beadwork dresses for themselves and children, and moccasins and shirts for their husbands, besides cooking for the family and teaching the children their proper worship of the Great Spirit.

The next morning there appeared on the bluff just at the break of day, and while most of the inmates of the teepees were in their deepest sleep, a part of the United States army under command of Colonel Baker, who in an undertone told his men to keep cool, aim to kill and spare none. Then he gave the command to fire. The first volley was very low in the lodges, and many of the sleeping inmates were killed in their beds.

The ones not killed in the first fire rushed out of their teepees not knowing what was happening — mostly women and children, many with babes in their arms — only to be shot down as they appeared in the open. Bear's Head, the Chief, came with a white man's certificate in his hand, waving it and calling frantically to stop firing on his women and children. The paper he so tragically held up and believed in for safety was from white officials showing that he was friendly and entitled to protection by the United States armies. But in this case it was useless — he was shot down like all the rest, while he was thus putting his faith in the white man and the white man's certificate of good character: both were shot down together.

Then the soldiers shot the wounded ones to put them out of misery. They tore down the teepees, piled the bodies together, with their firewood and household belongings on top of them, and set fire to the whole pile, including the bodies of women, children and the few men that were killed. The day previous the men of the camp had gone to the Sweetwater Hills on a grand buffalo-hunt, so there were only the old men and the Chief, besides the women and children, left to be massacred by the brave Baker and his troops.

Schultz was there some years after and states that "Everywhere scattered about in the long grass and brush, just where the wolves and foxes left them, gleamed the skulls and bones of those who had been so ruthlessly slaughtered." Official reports show that of the killed, fifteen were men of fighting age, eighteen old men and ninety women and fifty-five little children and infants in arms.

Curley, the Crow Scout, Brings News of the Custer Fight to the Steamer Far West

(*Drawing by Charles M. Russell*)

Chapter
15

The Custer Fight

Dinner over, Flying Hawk wished to sit on the open veranda in the clear pure air and see the sunset shadows grow slowly over the hills and valleys all about. Another pipe-smoke to get his mind centered on the old times, and after a short time of quiet he began to relate the incidents of the Custer fight:

"The Indians were camped along the west side of the Big Horn in a flat valley. We saw a dust but did not know what caused it. Some Indians said it was the soldiers coming. The Chief saw a flag on a pole on the hill.

"The soldiers made a long line and fired into our teepees among our women and children. That was the first we knew of any trouble. The women got their children by the hand and caught up their babies and ran in every direction.

"The Indian men got their horses and guns as quick as they could and went after the soldiers. Kicking Bear and Crazy Horse were in the lead. There was the thick timber and when they got

111

out of the timber there was where the first of the fight was.

"The dust was thick and we could hardly see. We got right among the soldiers and killed a lot with our bows and arrows and tomahawks. Crazy Horse was ahead of all, and he killed a lot of them with his war-club; he pulled them off their horses when they tried to get across the river where the bank was steep. Kicking Bear was right beside him and killed many too in the water.

"This fight was in the upper part of the valley where most of the Indians were camped. It was some of the Reno soldiers that came after us there. It was in the day just before dinner when the soldiers attacked us. When we went after them they tried to run into the timber and get over the water where they had left their wagons. The bank was about this high [twelve feet indicated] and steep, and they got off their horses and tried to climb out of the water on their hands and knees, but we killed nearly all of them when they were running through the woods and in the water. The ones that got across the river and up the hill dug holes and stayed in them.

"The soldiers that were on the hill with the pack-horses began to fire on us. About this time all the Indians had got their horses and guns and bows and arrows and war-clubs and they charged the soldiers in the east and north on top of the hill. Custer was farther north than these soldiers were then. He was going to attack the lower end of the village. We drove nearly all that got away from us down the hill along the ridge where another lot of soldiers were trying to make a stand.

"Crazy Horse and I left the crowd and rode down along the river. We came to a ravine; then we followed up the gulch to a place in the rear of the soldiers that were making the stand on the hill. Crazy Horse gave his horse to me to hold along with my horse. He crawled up the ravine to where he could see the soldiers. He shot them as fast as he could load his gun. They fell off their horses as fast as he could shoot. [Here the Chief swayed rapidly back and forth to show how fast they fell.] When they found they were being killed so fast, the ones that were left broke and ran as fast as their horses could go to some other soldiers that were further along the ridge toward Custer. Here they tried to make another stand and fired some shots, but we rushed them on along the ridge to where Custer was. Then they made another stand (the third) and rallied a few minutes. Then they went along the ridge and got with Custer's men.

"Other Indians came to us after we got most of the men at the ravine. We all kept after them until they got to where Custer was. There was only a few of them left then.

"By that time all the Indians in the village had got their horses and guns and watched Custer.

When Custer got nearly to the lower end of the camp, he started to go down a gulch, but the Indians were surrounding him, and he tried to fight. They got off their horses and made a stand but it was no use. Their horses ran down the ravine right into the village. The squaws caught them as fast as they came. One of them was a sorrel with white stocking. Long time after some of our relatives told us they had seen Custer on that kind of a horse when he was on the way to the Big Horn.

"When we got them surrounded the fight was over in one hour. There was so much dust we could not see much, but the Indians rode around and yelled the war-whoop and shot into the soldiers as fast as they could until they were all dead. One soldier was running away to the east but Crazy Horse saw him and jumped on his pony and went after him. He got him about half a mile from the place where the others were lying dead. The smoke was lifted so we could see a little. We got off our horses and went and took the rings and money and watches from the soldiers. We took some clothes off too, and all the guns and pistols. We got seven hundred guns and pistols. Then we went back to the women and children and got them together that were not killed or hurt.

"It was hard to hear the women singing the death-song for the men killed and for the wailing because their children were shot while they played in the camp. It was a big fight; the soldiers got just what they deserved this time. No good soldiers would shoot into the Indian's teepee where there were women and children. These soldiers did, and we fought for our women and children. White men would do the same if they were men.

"We did not mutilate the bodies, but just took the valuable things we wanted and then left. We got a lot of money but it was of no use.

"We got our things packed up and took care of the wounded the best we could, and left there the next day. We could have killed all the men that got into the holes on the hill, but they were glad to let us alone, and so we let them alone too. Rain-in-the-Face was with me in the fight. There were twelve hundred of us. Might be no more than one thousand in the fight. Many of our Indians were out on a hunt.

"There was more than one Chief in the fight, but Crazy Horse was leader and did most to win the fight along with Kicking Bear. Sitting Bull was right with us. His part in the fight was all good. My mother and Sitting Bull's wife were sisters; she is still living.

"The names of the Chiefs in the fight were: Crazy Horse, Sitting Bull, Lame Deer, Spotted Eagle and Two Moon. Two Moon led the Cheyennes. Gall and some other Chiefs were there but the ones I told you were the leaders. The story that white men told about Custer's heart being cut out is not true."

Indicating that he was through, the manuscript was carefully read over to him very slowly in order that he would not be confused as to the exact meaning of what it contained. When finished he gave his emphatic approval by hearty "How how, washta," and in his expert use of the sign language directed a pad be brought so that he could place his thumb-print to show that it was his own sealed document and final testimony on a subject about which white men have written countless and varied accounts, all of them being guesswork based upon circumstantial evidence, for no white man knows. There were none left to tell just what did occur and how. But Flying Hawk was there and he saw and knew. He was last of the survivors of that historic episode, and it is fortunate that coming generations could have a truthful and reliable account from him before he too had passed to the Happy Hunting Ground.

Chapter

16

Red Cloud

Rested and refreshed, Flying Cloud desired to talk about the cause of the Custer troubles.

He said that Red Cloud was one of their wisest men and knew what was best for his people; he had been their Chief for a long time; he tried to keep peace with the whites but it was no use — they would not stay out of the Indians' country, but came and took their gold and killed off all their game. This started the trouble, and the long bloody war with the soldiers came.

After the Custer fight and when the Indians were starving, Red Cloud made a speech about it, he said, and asked to have it read to him now. His host brought from the library a volume containing the talk to which the Chief referred, and it was carefully translated to him by Thunderbull by way of refreshing his memory. On completing this interpretation of Red Cloud's famous address, the Chief directed that it be included following his story of the Custer fight so that people would know why they killed Custer and his troopers. Also, it would tell why there was ghost dancing, and of the massacre at Wounded Knee.

RED CLOUD'S SPEECH

"I will tell you the reason for the trouble. When we first made treaties with the Government, our old life and our old customs were about to end; the game on which we lived was disappearing; the whites were closing around us, and nothing remained for us but to adopt their ways. The Government promised us all the means necessary to make our living out of the land, and to instruct us how to do it, and with abundant food to support us until we could take care of ourselves. We looked forward with hope to the time we could be as independent as the whites, and have a voice in the Government.

"The army officers could have helped better than anyone else but we were not left to them. An Indian Department was made with a large number of agents and other officials drawing large salaries — then came the beginning of trouble; these men took care of themselves but not of us. It was very hard to deal with the Government through them — they could make more for themselves by keeping us back than by helping us forward.

"We did not get the means for working our lands; the few things they gave us did little good.

"Our rations began to be reduced; they said we were lazy. That is false. How does any man of sense suppose that so great a number of people could get work at once unless they were at once supplied with the means to work and instructors enough to teach them?

"Our ponies were taken away from us under the promise that they would be replaced by oxen and large horses; it was long before we saw any, and then we got very few. We tried with the means we had, but on one pretext or another, we were shifted from one place to another, or were told that such a transfer was coming. Great efforts were made to break up our customs, but nothing was done to introduce us to customs of the whites. Everything was done to break the power of the real Chiefs.

"Those old men really wished their people to improve, but little men, so-called Chiefs, were made to act as disturbers and agitators. Spotted Tail wanted the ways of the whites, but an assassin was found to remove him. This was charged to the Indians because an Indian did it, but who set on the Indian? I was abused and slandered, to weaken my influence for good. This was done by men paid by the Government to teach us the ways of the whites. I have visited many other tribes and found that the same things were done among them; all was done to discourage us and nothing to encourage us. I saw men paid by the Government to help us, all very busy making money for themselves, but doing nothing for us.

"Now, do you suppose we saw all this? Of course we did, but what could we do? We were prisoners, not in the hands of the army but in the hands of robbers. Where was the army? Set to watch us but having no voice to set things right. They could not speak for us. Those who held us pretended to be very anxious about our welfare and said our condition was a great mystery. We tried to speak and clear up that mystery but were laughed at as children.

"Other treaties were made but it was all the same. Rations were again reduced and we were starving — sufficient food not given us, and no means to get it from the land. Rations were still further reduced; a family got for two weeks what was not enough for one week. What did we eat when that was gone? The people were desperate from starvation — they had no hope. They did not think of fighting; what good would it do; they might die like men but what would the women and children do?

"Some say they saw the Son of God. I did not see Him. If He had come He would do great things, as He had done before. We doubted it for we saw neither Him nor His works. Then General Crook came. His words sounded well but how could we know that a new treaty would be kept better than the old one?

For that reason we did not care to sign. He promised that his promise would be kept — he at least had never lied to us.

"His words gave the people hope; they signed. They hoped. He died. Their hope died with him. Despair came again. Our rations were again reduced. The white men seized our lands; we sold them through General Crook but our pay was as distant as ever.

"The men who counted [census] told all around that we were feasting and wasting food. Where did he see it? How could we waste what we did not have? We felt we were mocked in our misery; we had no newspaper and no one to speak for us. Our rations were again reduced.

"You who eat three times a day and see your children well and happy around you cannot understand what a starving Indian feels! We were faint with hunger and maddened by despair. We held our dying children and felt their little bodies tremble as their soul went out and left only a dead weight in our hands. They were not very heavy but we were faint and the dead weighed us down. There was no hope on earth. God seemed to have forgotten.

"Someone had been talking of the Son of God and said He had come. The people did not know; they did not care; they snatched at hope; they screamed like crazy people to Him for mercy; they caught at the promise they heard He had made.

"The white men were frightened and called for soldiers. We begged for life and the white men thought we wanted theirs; we heard the soldiers were coming. We did not fear. We hoped we could tell them our suffering and could get help. The white men told us the soldiers meant to kill us; we did not believe it but some were frightened and ran away to the Bad Lands. The soldiers came. They said: 'Don't be afraid — we come to make peace, not war.' It was true; they brought us food. But the hunger-crazed who had taken fright at the soldiers' coming and went to the Bad Lands could not be induced to return to the horrors of reservation life. They were called hostiles and the Government sent the army to force them back to their reservation prison."

Red Cloud's review of the great Sioux war as told by Flying Hawk was reduced to form after this and previous talks about his old friend, the famous leader and counselor. On many former occasions historic data had been assembled and notes made of the Chief's discussions and his judgment of the Great Chief of the Sioux in his contest with the Federal armies; he called him the Red Man's George Washington. All these notes were now read over to him, and what changes he desired made were made, together with present comments added, so that the whole was approved and thumb-printed, as he remarked that he would never talk of Red Cloud again. The signed statement included the following:

Samuel Bowles, editor of the Springfield Republican, in writing of his trip by stage across the continent in 1865, said "the testimony is universal in these states, that the whites have originated most of the trouble with the Indians — the great Oregon War of some years ago was clearly provoked by whites as a means of speculating in supplies for carrying on war against them — the lust of coarse white men for their women; the introduction of whiskey among them; abuse and maltreatment in various ways, are the origin of a good many Indian outrages, and these lead to wars of extermination — mean and sordid whites stir the Indian's blood, teach him the ways of mischief — but this is not necessary — if our Indian Department were both vigorously and wisely administered."

Careful study of the causes leading up to the Wounded Knee massacre proves conclusively that the white man was the aggressor there. All unbiased opinions of those on the ground, the men not of the war-party, agree:

That the whole matter has been brought about by a bad policy, and incompetency of some officials — the policy has been pursued to take lands of the Indians and not pay enough for them to keep the Indians from starving to death when dispossessed of their homes — rations were reduced, and lasted, even when conserved, but one half the period they were issued for — physicians said, in many cases, they died when taken sick, not so much from disease as from want of food.

Chapter 17

Wounded Knee

The old man being assured that Red Cloud's talk would be incorporated in his history, then said he wished to tell about the massacre of Indians by the white soldiers at Wounded Knee, where, he indicated as his belief, they carried out this slaughter in retaliation for the Custer affair, and proceeded:

"This was the last big trouble with the Indians and soldiers and was in the winter in 1890. When the Indians would not come in from the Bad Lands, they got a big army together with plenty of clothing and supplies and camp-and-wagon equipment for a big campaign; they had enough soldiers to make a round-up of all the Indians they called hostiles.

"The Government army, after many fights and loss of lives, succeeded in driving these starving Indians, with their families of women and gaunt-faced children, into a trap, where they could be forced to surrender their arms. This was on Wounded Knee creek, northeast of Pine Ridge, and here the Indians were surrounded by the soldiers, who had Hotchkiss machine guns along with them. There were about four thousand Indians in this big camp, and the soldiers had the machine guns pointed at them from all around the village as the soldiers formed a ring about the teepees so that Indians could not escape.

"The Indians were hungry and weak and they suffered from lack of clothing and furs because the whites had driven away all the game. When the soldiers had them all surrounded and they had their teepees set up, the officers sent troopers to each of them to search for guns and take them from the owners. If the Indians in the teepees did not at once hand over a gun, the soldier tore open their par-fleech trunks and bundles and bags of robes or clothes, looking for pistols and knives and ammunition. It was an ugly business, and brutal; they treated the Indians like they would torment a wolf with one foot in a strong trap; they could do this because the Indians were now in the white man's trap — and they were helpless.

"Then a shot was heard from among the Indian teepees. An Indian was blamed; the excitement began; soldiers ran to their stations; officers gave orders to open fire with the machine guns into the crowds of innocent men, women and children, and in a few minutes more than two hundred and twenty of them lay in the snow dead and dying. A terrible blizzard raged for two days, cover-

ing the bodies with Nature's great white blanket;
some lay in piles of four or five; others in twos or
threes or singly, where they fell, until the storm
subsided. When a trench had been dug of sufficient
length and depth to contain the frozen corpses,
they were collected and piled, like cord-wood, in
one vast icy tomb. While separating several stiffened forms which had fallen in a heap, two of
them proved to be women, and hugged closely to
their breasts were infant babes still alive after lying
in the storm for two days in twenty degrees below
zero weather.

"I was there and saw the trouble — but after
the shooting was over; it was all bad."

The host produced an old photograph showing the
bodies of the victims as they lay scattered and in bunches
over the bleak frozen grounds. The Chief looked at it and
immediately recognized the body of Big Foot, which lay
on top of a pile of the dead, face upward. Another photograph showing the trench being filled with the dead
also showed a number of army officers standing nearby.
The Chief readily recognized Frank Gruard, Buffalo
Bill, General Miles and Kicking Bear, his own brother.
He shook his head and said, "wahnitcha"— bad.

Wounded Knee followed the death of Sitting Bull,
and profuse reports of its justification fill the War Department files. But the old Chief was there, and repudiated much of the white man's stories about it. He
wished to correct this and, in the future, make history

books tell the truth about what happened there. He said:

"White man's books say it was the battle of Wounded Knee. It was a bloody massacre — like Washita, and Sand Creek, and the Pequot and Narragansett troubles. The white men didn't want to be bothered with Indians after they took their land from them, and so they stirred up excuse to cheat and rob them and make them mad, then put the soldiers on them and kill them all.

"The Indians had been starving because the crooked agents held the Government rations to sell and make money for themselves. The Indians went off the reservation to hunt; they had to have food; they did not want war; only something to keep their little ones and their women from dying of hunger. And then the army was sent to herd them like cattle and drive them back to their prison camp. Then for punishment, their rations were cut; many died for want of food, but crooked agents and politicians did nothing to help them. Then the war general promised to give them enough food if they would come in and surrender and Big Foot believed him. He brought his band, with all their women and children and ponies with their teepees and blankets; four thousand men, women and children; they made their village on Wounded Knee Creek. The soldiers were all around them with machine guns ready to shoot them if they tried to go away again.

"When the Indians got their teepees up and could keep their little children in the warm, the soldiers went to the teepees and began to take from the squaws, from their blankets and their robes and shawls, what they could find of knives, pistols or old guns which they had used in hunting. They were very rough when they went into the teepees; they did not ask for things, but broke open the squaws' bundles, tore their dresses open, broke their boxes of food, and turned the babies out of their hammocks; they swore at them and slapped them. Then when they were doing such things in his mother's teepee, a young man could no longer stand to see his family abused. He fought a trooper to throw him out; the soldier drew his revolver and shot at the boy and ran out and yelled. Soon other Indians ran to see what it was about. The soldiers ran up and made a great noise, then ran away to their company; the soldier company, joined to the next company, all to the next one, so they all made a great army in a big ring around the Indian camp ground.

"They got excited and soon the general ordered the Hotchkiss machine guns to fire into the crowd of Indians where they had gathered to see about the shot that was made by the trooper in the squaw's teepee. It was a big crowd of old men and women; some of these women had their papooses in their arms. The soldiers kept their quick fire cannons going until they had killed more than two

hundred of these harmless men and women; and
then they left the bodies where they fell in the
snow when it was twenty degrees below zero; they
left them there two days. When they found that
the ones who were left could not fight or get away,
the soldiers came with wagons and mules and
hauled the frozen bodies to a long trench which
they had dug in the hard ground; they piled the
bodies into the ditch like cords of wood and
covered them with clods and snow.

"When the soldiers came to load the bodies in
the wagons, they found a pile of them that had
fallen together in a heap; they pried and tore the
stiff bodies apart so they could lift them into the
wagon, and two of them were women in that pile.
When they got the bodies loose these two squaws
had their shawls wrapped around their breasts and
underneath each one's shawl was a live baby. The
army officer took them to his home; one of them
lived but a little while, but the other one lived; I
think she is living yet. This was the last white man
massacre of Indians.   The officers and soldiers
hated the Indians because they had won the fight
with Custer. I was in both of these affairs and saw
all that happened in each one; I know that the
whites were wrong in each one. I want the truth
to be printed as I have said all truth."

As the old Chief affixed his thumb-print to the above
statement his host told him of being at Wounded Knee

recently, when he tried to get a squaw to talk about it. But when the subject was mentioned to her, she broke into wailing the death-song, for she had seen it all; could not talk about it. The Chief's comment was a sad look and one word: "How."

Chapter 18

Crazy Horse

Historians and students of the American Indian generally acknowledge that Crazy Horse was perhaps the greatest of Indian warriors. As time passes, his name and fame draw more and more respect from Indians and whites alike. It was his position as War Chief and his outstanding generalship that held the United States armies at bay throughout the great Sioux war, beginning with Red Cloud's destruction of the Bozeman Trail forts and garrisons, to the annihilation of Custer's army at Little Big Horn. Though nine years the senior of Flying Hawk, Crazy Horse and the Hawk were constant close friends and associates; and they were cousins.

In former years the host had secured much information from Flying Hawk regarding Crazy Horse, from which notes were made. Now it seemed that as there would be no future chance to gather more data from Flying Hawk, it meant a cross examination to get from him new material on the Great Chief's life and personal characteristics. Assembling all former notes about him, a life-story of the noted War Chief was constructed accordingly; it suited the old man's specifications, and at its close he put his thumb-print, to show his approval of what he had known about him, as written and read over by the interpreter. Patched together in the best manner possible in the limited time given for it, the statement follows:

Crazy Horse was a great leader. White men who contended with him and knew him well, spoke of him in the highest terms. His word was not called in question by either white men or red; he was honored by his own people and respected by his enemies. Though they hunted and persecuted him, they murdered him because they could not conquer him.

He was born in Southern Dakota Territory in 1844, and his parents gave him the best of training as a youth. He grew to manhood, when it was said of him that he was "uncommonly handsome, of imposing stature and an Apollo in symmetry — a splendid example of refinement and grace" — "modest and courteous always, and a born leader of men."

In his boyhood days there were few white men to be seen, but when met, they were extended a hand of friendship. His name derived from a personality like a high-spirited and uncontrolled horse — hence crazy or wild horse; and he was an expert horseman. When sixteen years old, he was taken along with a war-party headed by Hump, a famed Sioux Chief, on a campaign against the Gros Ventres. In the fight which came, the

Chief's horse was shot; the enemy rushed in to scalp him while struggling for release from the fallen animal, when Crazy Horse drove his pony alongside and rescued Hump, both escaping on the boy's horse.

When still under twenty, in a winter hunt alone, he brought in ten buffalo tongues for a council feast, then being held by old men of the tribe; these were all taken with bow and arrows.

Of Crazy Horse, it is well known that he never would take a scalp from his fallen enemy; he struck the body with a switch — coupstick — to show that he neither cared for their weapons, nor cared to waste his. He never dressed in gaudy regalia, feathers and paint and beads; never took part in public demonstrations or dances; he was not an orator, and was never known to make a speech; and he never sat for a photograph; yet as a War Chief, he won every battle that he undertook. Once he was attacked in camp when he had his women and children with them, yet was able to extricate them with great credit and little loss.

As the youth came to manhood there were rumbles of trouble with the whites, and soon the great Sioux war came on. Spotted Tail, then Chief of the Tetons, and Red Cloud, with other leaders, decided there must be a stand made or they would be annihilated, in the grand rush of white hordes who were building roads and railroads into their hunting grounds. At a Grand Council in 1866 it was decided to fight, and when the Government built Fort Phil Kearny in the heart of their buffalo range, Crazy

Horse took the lead to drive out the invaders. His attack on the Fetterman party at the timber-cutting showed that he was a master of strategy.

Thereafter the war became general and Crazy Horse was recognized as a formidable antagonist by the Government's armies; and the allied tribes acknowledged him as leader in carrying out the Council's program of campaigns to fight the troops. For years his band was followed — in winter and in summer; the soldiers tracked them as they would trail wild animals to the lair; surrounded and struck them while asleep in their teepees; every effort of a Government with unlimited resources was exerted to capture or exterminate Crazy Horse and his people, but without success.

Baffled on every turn, the Government organized a formidable army of four grand divisions: Crook to advance from the south at Fort Laramie into the Powder River country; Gibbon to come from the west, and Custer's cavalry to join Terry's division on the Yellowstone; and all to close in on the allied tribes who were believed to be in the game country on the headwaters of the Rosebud and Big Horn Rivers.

Crook had reached the head of Rosebud with his army in mid-July when contact was made with the Indians. Here Crazy Horse turned on him and gave him such a fight that he turned back; and his army never made the junction with Terry, Gibbon and Custer as he set out to do.

From here Crazy Horse took his band over the divide

to Little Big Horn to get with Sitting Bull's camp, and where they hoped to be let alone. But this was not to be, for in the meantime, Terry had received Custer's troops and sent his cavalry division up the Rosebud Valley, expecting to find the Indians somewhere near its head. They crossed to the Little Big Horn, and discovered their camps along its west side. The other divisions were not there to help, and Custer decided to go it alone. Reno was ordered to open attack on the camp, upstream, while Custer himself followed down the east side to attack them where the villages were more concentrated. He was not aware that Crazy Horse had stopped his expected aid from Crook a week before and that he was now here and ready to lead his warriors to his own army's extermination.

Crazy Horse and Flying Hawk were at the upper village when Reno's troop formed a line after dismounting, and opened fire on the teepees where only women and children were. It was the first intimation that these two Indians had that soldiers were in the vicinity.

The Indians could have wiped out Reno's and all the rest of the soldiers, just as they did Custer's troops, if they had been so disposed; but as Reno had dug in and was willing to quit, the red folks decided to leave them there, went to look after their women, children and old people who had not been killed in the first assault when no one was with them to defend them, and packed up their belongings and left the bloody scene.

Sitting Bull, with his people, went to Canada to

escape the storm of shot and shell which was sure to be rained on them, after the story of Custer's defeat became known in the east; but Crazy Horse stayed on, defiant of his enemies, who now, more than ever, recognized his capabilities for taking care of himself and his persecuted people. Reduced from the scattering of the separate tribes, his people suffered greatly from lack of food in the severe winter which followed, and the persistent trailing by guerilla warfare troops, which were furnished with transport, telegraph and the best equipment, while he had women and children with him, and had to provide food, warm clothing and shelter for them at all times. It was like a pack of hungry wolves on the track of a strayed mother sheep and her lambs!

Crazy Horse decided to accede to the plea of the reservation authorities that he come in and accept their promise of supplies and fair treatment. Therefore, in July of '77 he, with several thousands of his own and other Chiefs' followers, surrendered and came in to the reservation, with the distinct condition that the Government would hear and grant his claims.

Instead, General Crook immediately recognized Spotted Tail as the head Chief, knowing that he had turned against his own people and favored anything the army stood for, and might be depended on to control the late prisoners with military severity. This was received with bitterness by practically all the reservation Indians. Failure to provide food and supplies as promised soon stirred up contention between the Spotted Tail adherents and the great number of surrendered people.

They of the agency power blamed Crazy Horse; he had been their leader and unconquered enemy of the army forces, and might lead them again to liberty from their unsatisfactory position if the surrendered horde at any time so decided. So a conspiracy was formed to assassinate the War Chief. It was discovered by friends of Crazy Horse, who told him; he replied by saying "only cowards and murderers" — and went about his daily routine.

At the time this tale was brought to him, his wife was critically ill and he took her to her parents, at Spotted Tail Agency, some miles north, and during his absence on this mission of love and kindness, his enemies spread the report that he had left to organize another war. Scouts were sent to arrest him; he was overtaken while in the wagon with his sick wife and one other person; he was not arrested but permitted to deliver his patient into the care of her parents.

Crazy Horse returned voluntarily, not suspecting any immediate treachery. When he reached the agency, a guard directed him to enter the guard-house. His cousin, Touch-the-Cloud, called to him "They are going to put you in the guard-house!" He stopped suddenly to say, "Another white man's trick — let me go"; but he was held by guards and police, and when he tried to free himself from their grasp, a soldier stepped from behind and ran a bayonet through his kidney. He died during the night while his father sang the death-song over his prostrate body. His father and mother and neighbors carried the body to a secret cave, saying it must not be polluted by the touch of any white man. Thus was murdered one of the greatest generals of modern times, at the age of thirty-three.

Amongst the old papers regarding the death of Crazy Horse is the following statement signed by Flying Hawk at that time:

"I was present at the death of Crazy Horse; he was my cousin; his father and his two wives and an uncle of Crazy Horse took the body away, and no one knows today where he is buried. Several years later, they went to see how the body was, and when the ground was removed, they found the bones, and they were petrified; they never would tell where they buried him."

Signed: Flying Hawk Chief.

By his thumb-print.

Witness: Thunderbull

Other previous statements by the Chief about Crazy Horse follow:

"I have been in nine battles with Crazy Horse; won them all. Crazy Horse was quiet and not inclined to associate with others; he was in the front of every battle; he was the greatest leader of our tribe; he told me this story once:

"'I was sitting on a hill or rise, and something touched me on the head; I felt for it and found it was a bit of grass. I took it to look at; there was a trail nearby and I followed it; it led to water; I went into the water; there the trail ended and I sat down in the water; I was nearly out of breath; I started to rise out of the water, and when I came out I was born by my mother. When I was born I could know and see and understand for a time, but afterwards went back to it as a baby; then I grew up naturally — at the age of seven I began to learn, and when twelve began to fight enemies. That was the reason I always refused to wear any war-dress; only a bit of grass in the hair; that was why I always was successful in battles. The first fight was with the Shoshones; the Shoshones were chasing the Sioux; I, with my younger brother riding double; two of the Shoshones came for us; we started to meet them; I killed one of them, took his horse; we jumped on him, my brother and I double, and escaped.'

"Crazy Horse was much alone when not in a fight or on travel or on a hunt; he was quiet and never told stories, but he was the first in every kind of trouble; he was married but had no children; his younger brother was on a campaign in the country about which is Utah, and was killed there by some settlers who were having trouble with some Indians there. When Crazy Horse learned that his brother was killed, he left the camp and took his wife, and nobody could find where he went. For a long time he was gone. He went to the place where his brother was killed, and camped in the woods, where he could see the settlement, but the thick woods protected his teepee from view. Here he stayed for nine days; every morning he got up and would stand and look; when he saw some enemy he shot him, until he had killed enough to satisfy him; then went back home."

Chapter 19

Sitting Bull

As the famed Sitting Bull was his uncle, Flying Hawk wished to talk about him, and told of the suffering that followed the removal of the Minnesota bands to Crow Creek in 1863. There the young man learned of the terrible injustices and frightful sufferings that his people were subjected to at the hands of the national government through its grafting agents and hordes of unconscionable politicians. The outrageous treatment of these innocent and confiding natives, whose rich land along the Mississippi was confiscated by the land-speculators, and then "purchased" by treaty, but never paid for, as usual, and the owners thrust far out into the barren sand hills and allowed to starve and die of helplessness and foul disease — left an indelible hate in the heart of Sitting Bull against the white race.

Sitting Bull was a natural leader, but it was after the ruthless breaking by the whites of the treaty of 1868 that he gained wide prominence. He visited Washington with Red Cloud and Spotted Tail, where they were entertained by President Grant.

At a council on Powder River he made a speech to his associates which indicated the range of his oratory and intellect. He said:

"Behold, my brothers, the Spring has come; the earth has received the embraces of the sun and we shall soon see the results of that love!

"Every seed is awakened; and so has all animal life; it is through this mysterious power that we too have our being, and we therefore yield to our neighbors, even to our animal neighbors, the same right as ourselves, to inhabit this land.

"Yet hear me, people, we have now to deal with another race — small and feeble when our fathers first met them, but now great and overbearing. Strangely enough, they have a mind to till the soil, and the love of possession is a disease with them. These people have made many rules that the rich may break, but the poor may not; they have a religion in which the poor worship, but the rich will not. They take tithes from the poor and weak to support the rich and those who rule. They claim this mother of ours, the earth, for their own and fence their neighbors away; they deface her with their buildings and their refuse. That nation is like a spring freshet that overruns its banks and destroys all who are in its path.

"We cannot dwell side by side. Only seven years ago we made a treaty by which we were assured that the buffalo country should be left to us forever. Now they threaten to take that from us. My brothers, shall we submit, or shall we say to them: 'First kill me before you take possession of my fatherland.'"

Observing a photograph of Sitting Bull which hung on the wall, Flying Hawk remarked that he was the brains of the fighting forces, but the fighting was led by Crazy Horse, his young War Chief. This was after Red Cloud had agreed to peace and retired from active leadership. He said that Sitting Bull was always a fair fighter and never killed any women or children.

Mention of Sitting Bull's life in Canada brought from the old Chief the story of a visit he made to Sitting Bull's camp in Wood Mountain long years after the Great Chief's death. He said that when Sitting Bull left for Canada with the hostiles, seven families, who were not of his band, were missed from the reservation; no one knew where they were and they were given up as killed by the whites.

Then about forty years passed and Flying Hawk heard that a band of Indians were living at Sitting Bull's old camping ground in Canada. He went to visit them. He found that they numbered five hundred, and they lived in teepees just as the Indians lived in the old days, and that they had all descended from the original seven lost families. He said they were fine, healthy and happy, and their hair reached below the knee.

While talking about Sitting Bull, the old Chief referred to his speech about treaties made with the whites. On examination, the library had a volume containing the speech, which was read to the old man by the interpreter. He asked to have it placed in his history so that people would know the truth about the way Indians were abused and cheated. The speech follows:

"What treaty that the white man kept has the red man broken? Not one.

"What treaty that the white man ever made with us have they kept? Not one.

"When I was a boy the Sioux owned the land; the sun rose

and set on their country; they sent ten thousand horsemen to battle! Where are the warriors today? Who slew them? Where are our lands? Who owns them?

"What white man can say I ever stole his lands or a penny of his gold? Yet they say I am a thief! What white woman, however lonely, was ever a captive or insulted by me? Not one, yet they say I am a bad Indian. What white man has ever seen me drunk? Who has ever come to me hungry and went unfed? Who has ever seen me beat my wives or abuse my children? What law have I ever broken? Is it wrong for me to love my own? Is it wicked for me because my skin is red — because I am a Sioux — because I was born where my fathers lived — because I would die for my people and my country?"

Red Cloud had said of Sitting Bull that he "was nothing but what the white man made him. He was a conceited man who never did anything great, but wanted to get into notice; white men who had something to make by it, encouraged him and used him. When they made him as great as they could, they killed him to get a name by it. If he was a little man, he was a man, and should not have been murdered uselessly. The Indian Department has almost destroyed us."

At this time Father Craft wrote of the killing of Sitting Bull:

They are in every way abused, mocked and discouraged. Instead of wards they are victims of unscrupulous politicians who benefit by their misery; just as the tree can be traced from its smallest branch to its roots, so can the Indian troubles be traced to starvation and misery of the Indians.

Flying Hawk said he was there through all this time and saw it just as Red Cloud had said it was, and much of the things they wrote about was worse than they told about it.

As Sitting Bull was known to both the host and

Flying Hawk, it was a more or less delicate subject to talk about; yet both had a more liberal opinion of him than was expressed by Red Cloud, Flying Hawk having known him intimately and having been closely associated with him through his lifetime.

Flying Hawk succeeded Red Cloud as Chief and for more than fifty years he possessed the old tribal peace pipe, turned over to him by Sitting Bull after the Custer troubles, when leaving for Canada. This pipe, the Chief said, had been handed down for many generations, and was three hundred, perhaps four hundred, years old, and was the one used in all important ceremonials and in treaty-making with Government Commissions affecting the Sioux. His host and old friend would hold it here-after. Without further comment, the Chief went to his travel sack, got out the old pipe bowl of redstone, placed the stem in it and handed it over, saying simply: "The white chief's to hold."

Asked how he regarded Bull's behavior at the Custer fight, the old man said it was all good. Bull was not in the fight, he said, but he was one of the main advisors in the strategy before, and again after the fight was over. He was a great leader and very smart and wise. He said that he had been at the old Chief's grave not long ago, and found it grown over with weeds and in a neglected condition. He felt that a lowdown murder had been committed by the Government in the way Buffalo Bill and Jim McLaughlin had been interfered with:

"The Great Chief would have willingly done

anything that McLaughlin, the agent, or Colonel
Cody asked him to do — there was no need to
arrest him, he was not doing wrong. He was celebrating the coming of the new Christ who was to
restore the buffalo so that his people could once
more have peace and plenty, instead of the persecution, hunger, disease and death that con-
fronted them."

Turning the inquiry to Sitting Bull, the Chief was
asked his opinion of his uncle as an orator.

"He was a strong speaker just like any white
senator; he was a good politician; white politicians
are only 'medicine men' for their people — most
time crazy."

As the host had been possessed of the Great Chief's
pony when in his country in the middle eighties, he asked
Flying Hawk if he remembered Bull's dun colored horse;
he did, he said, and that it was Sitting Bull's favorite
buffalo-pony until the herds were all killed off by the
hide-hunters in 1883-84. Then he traded him off.

It may interest the reader to read comments made at
the time of Sitting Bull's death. Perhaps no better portrait
was ever made of him than the pen-picture by his close
friend, W. H. H. Murray, whose tribute was printed in
the *New York World* shortly after the assassination. Since
the article is not readily accessible and had been referred
to by Flying Hawk on former visits as "all truth" it is
liberally quoted from:

The land-grabbers wanted the Indian lands. The lying, thieving agents wanted silence touching past thefts and immunity to continue their thieving. The renegades from their people, the Indians, wanted opportunity to show their power over a man who despised them as renegades, and whom therefore, they hated. The public opinion of the frontier — outgrowth of ignorance, credulity and selfish greed — more than assented to a plan to rid the country of one who, while he lived, so great was he in fame and in fact, must forever stand as a reminder of wars past and a threat of wars to come. Out of all these and other causes peculiar to the condition of things there localized — some accidental, some deplorable, others famous and infamous, was born, as Milton's death was born, from Satan and Sin, the plot to kill him. And, so he was murdered!

I knew this man; knew him in relation to high office among his people, and in his elements as a man. As to his office or rank, I honored him. He filled a station older than human records; as a man, I admired him. He represented in person, the manners, and in mind and heroism of his spirit, the highest type of a race, which in many ways and rare virtues, stands peer to the noblest races in the world. As to his rank or official station, we whites called him "medicine man"; it is a name that does not name. . . . Sitting Bull was a prophet, not a war chief, to his people . . . by virtue of his office, old as custom and tradition, this man . . . was counselor of chiefs — the Warwick behind the throne — stronger than the throne, the oracle of mysteries and of knowledge hidden from the mass; hidden ever from the chiefs; to whose words of advice and authority, all listened as the last and highest expression of wisdom.

Such was Sitting Bull as to his office, as interpreted and understood from a standpoint of knowledge of religion, the traditions and the superstitions of his people. That he was faithful to his high office, all knew. He was in fact the counselor of chiefs; that as Joshua did to Moses, so he in hour of battle was lost or won. He lived as he died, a red man true to his office and his race; that leaf of laurel none can deny to his fame — not even his renegade murderers. But no office is so great as the man who fills it greatly, and this man was greater as a man, than he was even as a prophet.

I met him often; I studied him closely, as one of intelligence studies the type of a race — of a departing race — and knew him well. And this I say of him: he was a Sioux of the Sioux, a red man of red men. In his race, in his physique, in manners, in virtues, in faults he stood incarnate. In face, he was the only man I ever saw who resembled Gladstone — large featured, thoughtfully grave, reflective, reposeful, when unexcited. In wrath, his countenance was a collection of unexploded or exploding thunder — the awful embodiment of measureless passion and power.

In conversation, he was deliberate, the user of few words, but suave and low-voiced. In moments of social relaxation he was companionable, receptive of humor, a genial host or a pleasant guest. In his family, gentle, affectionate and not opposed to merriment. When sitting in council, his deportment was a model; grave, deliberate, courteous to opponent, patient and kind to men of lesser mind.

In pride, he was equal to his rank and race, a rank to him, level with a Pope's, and a race the oldest and bravest in the world. Of vanity I never saw one trace in him. I would couple to word with Gladstone or Webster as quickly as with him. He was never overdressed. He wore the insignia of his office as a king his robes or a judge his gown. In eating, he was temperate; from spirituous drinks, he was an abstainer. His word, once given as true as a bond; he was a born diplomat; no foe ever fathomed his thoughts. I have watched him by the hour when I knew his heart was hot with wrath, but neither from his eye nor lip nor cheek, nostril or sinewy hand might one get a hint of the storm raging within. There was no surface to him; he was the embodiment of depth.

Was he eloquent? What is eloquence? Men tell me that Mr. Depew is eloquent, and that New Yorkers go wild with the glasses in front of them, when Mr. Choate is speaking. I have read their words; their eloquence is not that of the great Sioux Prophet.

Here are some of his words, you may compare them with your orator's best:

"You tell me of the Mohawks. My father knew them. They demanded tribute of them. The Sioux laughed. They went to meet them; ten thousand horsemen. The Mohawks saw them coming, made them a feast and returned home. You tell me of the Abenakas — they are our forefathers and the forefathers of all red men. They were the men of the Dawn; they came from the east; they were born in the morning of the world; they rocked the cradle of our race."

"What treaty that the whites have kept has the red man broken? Not one. What treaty that the white man ever made with us have they kept? Not one. When I was a boy the Sioux owned the world; the sun rose and set on their land; they sent ten thousand men to battle. Where are the warriors today? Who slew them? Where are our lands? Who owns them? What white man can say I ever stole his land or a penny of his money? Yet, they say I am a thief. What white woman, however lonely, was ever captive or insulted by me? Yet, they say I am a bad Indian. What white man has ever seen me drunk? Who has ever come to me hungry and went unfed? Who has ever seen me beat my wives or abuse my children? What law have I broken? Is it wrong for me to love my own? Is it wicked for me because my skin is red? Because I am a Sioux; because I was born where my father lived; because I would die for my people and my country?

"They tell you that I murdered Custer. It is a lie. I am not a war chief. I was not in the battle that day. His eyes were blinded that he could not see. He was a fool and rode to his death. He made the fight, not I. Whoever tells you that I killed the Yellow Hair is a liar!"

But why tell more of this man? Does this generation love justice enough to ask that it be shown to the red man? Have not we, as a people fixed the brutal maxim in our language, that the only good Indian is a dead one? We laugh at the saying as a joke, but the cheeks of our descendants will redden with shame when they read the coarse brutality of our wit.

I read that the great Sioux was dead — that he was set upon in midst of his family, with his wives and children and relatives around him; that he had committed no overt act of war; that he was simply — so far as known — moving himself, his kith and kin from the midst of cold, hunger and peril, and that while doing this, a company of Indians — yclept Indian police — many of them despised as renegades from his own tribe, and enemies of his, under cover of the United States flag and backed by a company of United States cavalry — placed suspiciously near, to see that the renegades from his tribe should not fail in killing him; they went to kill him — and killed him. And I said, understanding the circumstances better than some — I said, "that is murder." And then, I read in a great journal that "everybody is well satisfied" with his death; and I cried out against the saying as I did against the deed. I read that they buried his body like a dog's — without funeral rites, without tribal wail, with no solemn song or act. That is the deed of today. That is the best that this generation has to give to this noble historic character, this man who in his person ends the line of aboriginal sanctities, older than the religion of Christian or of Jew. Very well. So let it stand for the present. But there is a generation coming that will reverse this judgment of ours. Our children shall build monuments to those whom we stoned — and those whom we killed will be counted by future generations as among the historic characters of a continent.

Chapter
20

Flying Hawk's Appraisal

To learn the opinion of Flying Hawk with regard to noted Indians, he was asked to tell what he knew of the following men: Joseph, the Nez Perce, Roman Nose, Captain Jack, American Horse and Afraid-of-His-Horses; and Geronimo the Apache — all of his own period though of different tribes and widely separated sections of the country.

Of Geronimo, he said that he was a low born fellow and had little training; lived in the barrens, ate snakes and jack-rabbits, but was faithful to his own people and a good fighter. The Mexicans were the same kind of people and they were always hunting each other. The Mexicans found him away one day, and burned his wigwam and killed his squaw and children; then he started out to kill everybody he met and got his friends to join him in raiding the whole territory. The Government sent troops to catch him; they had a hard time of it, but finally got him, and sent him to prison. "I didn't like him," the Chief finished.

Of Roman Nose, he had a better report to make. He considered him a great leader of his people and a brave fighter; that he had not been treated fair by the soldiers, and fought only for them and for his people's hunting grounds and their liberty. All Cheyennes were brave, he said. If they had not shot Roman Nose early in the fight at Arickaree, the Indians would have won that fight, for it was a fair daylight battle, and the Indians were right.

Captain Jack was hung as a renegade and murderer — he would not trust the white man's flag of truce and his flowery promises. He remembered Osceola, Pontiac and the many other red leaders who had been so led to their doom. The Modocs had been robbed, cheated and driven from their homes by the whites; they only fought for their rights as any good white men would do.

Afraid-of-His-Horses was a fine fellow and a brave Sioux Chief. He was like Crazy Horse and fought the soldiers in many battles of the Indians' wars of that time and was always in the front. He was not quiet like Crazy was, and he wore the war bonnet like the rest of the Chiefs, and he had his photograph made in full regalia and now we can see what he looked like, but we cannot show what Crazy Horse was like. He was a great horseman and could beat in races, and always won in fights with the Crows because they were afraid of his horses and that is how he got his name. "I knew 'Fraid and liked him; we were friends; we sometimes went on war parties, and had war dances together good many times."

Chief Joseph was a better general than any white generals of this Government; they could not whip him. They wanted to take his land and put the people on a reservation because their home on the fine pasture valleys in Washington and Oregon country suited the white settlers. The Indians refused to give it up. Soldiers came to force them to leave their homes so the cattle men could have it. Joseph left for Canada, where the Government was fair to the Indians; the soldiers followed to arrest them. For fifteen hundred miles the army chased Joseph and his bedraggled tribe of women and children; attacked them when asleep in their teepees after an all-day's exhausting travel over rocky travois trails, their ponies loaded with camp equipment and the women weighed down with papooses strapped to backs and little ones clinging to their skirts. Believing that he was over the boundary line and safe from further interference, Joseph made camp at Bear Paw Mountain; but because he had no maps, it proved that he was still within the American limits, and here with the combined military operations of Generals Howard and Miles he was attacked and captured after many of these innocent and patriotic natives had been killed. Joseph, like all great native leaders, was the victim of the Government's broken faith as the conditions of his surrender were at once violated.

American Horse, and his band, including women and children, were driven about in the bleak Bad Lands of Dakota until, crazed with fear, they sought refuge and were surrounded by Crook's army, when volleys of musketry were sent into their hiding place without regard for women and children there. When the wails of frantic mothers became more than the hardened soldiers could withstand, the grizzly general ordered a truce. He called on the women to surrender and bring out the little ones from the abandoned wolf-den in the ravine, where they had sought refuge from their merciless pursuers. Along with the women and children came old American Horse; he held his gun butt foremost in token of his willingness to give up. He had been shot in the groin; his squaws had tied their blankets about his wound to hold back the protruding entrails. Thus he was marched to the camp, where the surgeon pronounced his wound mortal. In the midst of the chanting of the death-songs of these terror-stricken women, the old warrior died in the hands of his captors.

Before the body of this great Chief was stiffened in death, Captain Jack, the scout — a friend of both host and visitor — was the swift messenger sent to Laramie to telegraph the news of the "great victory" over the enemy at Slim Buttes. Had it been reversed, it would have been called by the whites a terrible massacre, Flying Hawk said.

Speaking of former visits at the Wigwam, the old Chief was told of Plenty Coups having been a visitor a few years before, and that he enjoyed looking at the personal belongings of his old enemies, the Sioux. He remarked when looking at Rain-in-the-Face's war coat, that he was with a war-party once that tried to capture a lot of horses from the Sioux, and were chased back by Rain's band; he said Rain was a brave fellow when he was young, but when he got old, he drank too much firewater.

The old Chief said he knew Plenty Coups, but did not like him because he was a Crow and had helped Custer bring the soldiers to the Greasy Grass camp to fight the Sioux where the soldiers had no right to come. He said he had killed a good many Crows in long ago fights, and had lots of scalp dances over their long hair when they came back after a battle with them.

Asked how he regarded Reno's part in the Custer fight, he said that Reno began the fight by shooting into the teepees where there were only the women, old men and little children; no one but a coward would do such a thing! When the Indians went after Reno, they all ran away; they would not stand up and fight, but ran away like children. The white people's history tells that there were six thousand Indians for Custer to fight; that is not true; there were not more than one thousand or one thousand two hundred!

In telling stories of old days, the host related one which was told him by James T. Gardiner, a prominent geologist in early work of the United States Geological Survey. His survey party was attacked by Sioux and only by the sudden appearance of their supply wagon, they escaped being scalped. As the incident occurred in 1861, the Chief said he was not in the war-party because he was only nine then, but that if he had been a little older he would have been, and then they would have had a scalp dance over my friend Gardiner's hair.

Gardiner attended a Grand Council at which Washakie was to be the principal speaker and great interest was manifested by the Government representatives. All details were carefully arranged for his reception as he was to reply to the pleas of the eastern orators who for two days had advocated the adoption of agricultural pursuits by the big Chief's people. A banquet had been prepared, and everyone was anxiously awaiting the ceremony. When the audience had gathered in a circle with the dignitaries on benches and the natives on blankets spread on the ground surrounded by teepees, the Chief came dressed in his finest regalia and walked majestically into the middle space reserved for him and throwing his ornamented mantle from his shoulders, he signed for attention. Everyone was at attention; the Chief raised his right hand in lordly gesture and said: "God dam a potato" — and walked away.

Flying Hawk said he was not present at this Council, but he knew Washakie, the Shoshone, and that was just like he would do; he was too smart for the white fellows.

When questioned as to whom, amongst the military white people he knew, he held in highest regard, the Chief considered for some time, and then gave his answer:

"Crook was a good soldier but he was not a good general. Brooke was a kind and honest general, but they were not big enough to fight Red Cloud and Crazy Horse. Sheridan was a hard general; he was like Custer and said no Indians were good. Some of the agents were good men but they all were for making money for themselves. McLaughlin was all right but he could not do what he wanted because the high officers would not let him. Miles tried to do right sometimes, but he was bossed by Washington and did much to keep the Indians mad; he was wrong when Joseph surrendered at Bear Paw fight; Joseph was much bigger general; he never should have been sent to prison. Buffalo Bill was pretty tough with the Indians when he was a young fellow, but turned when he got older and was a friend of us until he died in 1917; we had a big meeting at his grave — about a hundred Indians went. Wild Bill Hickock was a good shot but no good, only gambled. Calamity Jane was a little tough but she was kind to us and all poor people."

Asked if he knew any of the Presidents, he said he had met every President since Garfield; he liked Theodore Roosevelt best for he was a neighbor in their country; he said Harrison did not treat them right in the uprising of 1890 when they were starving.

Suddenly the Chief asked if this town was the birthplace of Tom Mix and being answered in the affirmative, he said he knew Tom Mix, and thought he was a good rider. He was then told that it was also the home town of Johnny J. Jones, the great showman, and he said he knew Johnny Jones too, along with all the great showmen of the times; he said that this must be a good country to make such good fellows.

Flying Hawk was a radio fan and listened in with great interest. He remarked to the interpreter their manner of hurry communication in the early times. Properly translated, it was to describe the smoke signals, the buffalo "signs" and the sun-glass. They had a system of signals where, under certain conditions, messages were conveyed through sounds made by striking stones, shooting arrows and guns. Their expert runners, however, performed wonderful feats of rapid and long-distance communication, when it was a tribal necessity.

He said that with the radio, the airplanes, the automobiles and poison gas, the white people would kill themselves all off, and in the future there would be only the reds and the blacks and yellow people left in the world. If they can drop gas into a big city and kill all the people there, or blow up the railroads so no food can be sent to the ones that live in a city, they would soon starve.

"If the white people would live like the Indians lived, long ago, they could live for all time in this country, but now it is made so they cannot live that way but have to live in the fast way; and they do not work and get a living and they cannot go out and kill buffaloes to live now. Soon there will not be any more good ground to raise corn and squash for all to live on; the Indian way was the best way!"

Chiefs Flying Hawk (Age 59) and Iron Tail
(Age 60) with the Author and His Son
(Photo 1911)

Chief Flying Hawk
(Shortly before his death in 1931)

Chapter

21

Back to the Land of His Fathers

It was Sunday. Flying Hawk's leave of absence was about up and his visit to his white brother was coming to an end. The old man had arisen with the sun and taken a long walk in the woods to see the squirrels and hear the birds sing, he said.

He had taken especial care in arranging his toilet — an elk-tooth ornamented vest; the pink shell neck-piece; his best coat and bead-fringed trousers and moccasins. With his big tweezers, he had held his pocket-mirror close while he extracted such stray hair as might show in his face or chin; it was his morning shave. His long hair had been let down and carefully oiled with bear's grease. He was ready for breakfast.

When the family and guests were seated, the Chief signified that he wished grace to be said. The preacher's son Dick responded; he said: "God bless our food and fill our hearts with love, Amen." The Chief smiled approval, and then said he wished to go to church.

After breakfast the car was brought around, loaded to

capacity, and the old Chief, in full dress and just a little paint on his face to cover wrinkles, took place beside his host for the trip of two miles to the big Catholic edifice on State Street in the city's First Ward. Throughout the services the Chief responded with dignity to every detail of the long and solemn ceremony — and it may be said too that he attracted the gaze of everyone present. When formal service ended, the popular Father McGivney came to take his hand in welcome and gave his blessing, but it was long before the Chief was permitted to take leave of friends and neighbors gathered about him to shake hands.

The Chief was visibly agitated and frequently referred to his disappointment in having to go. He said he would not likely ever come again; he felt that he would soon go to join his friends in the Sand Hills. There were many other things he would like to talk about, when the white men had killed Indians without good reason, but he had not time to speak of the Pavonia massacre, and the Gnadenhutten massacre, the Conestoga massacre and many other cases of brutal mass-killing of natives when there was no just cause for it.

He said that Indians had no chance because the whites were cowards and would not meet the Indian face to face and fight like men, but hid behind trees and shot with powder and bullets a long way off. The Indian had to come close and shoot with a bow and arrow or fight with a knife; which one was the brave? he challenged.

And now the old Chief had "talked enough," he said, and was ready to go on the long trip to the Black Hills, where he would soon lie down for the long sleep. Just now he was feeling better. In his travel sack he had the doctor's certificate, and a letter to be handed the manager of the show. With a last look out over the landscape which had become so familiar, a final handclasp with host and family, the old man climbed into the motor car which was to speed him on his way west — back to the land of his fathers.

Appendix

The Sioux Calendar

Flying Hawk and his host had held long talks about the Sioux religion and their way of keeping track of time. The old Chief had prepared, with the assistance of his agency officials and the teachers at the Indian schools, the authentic calendar of the Sioux, covering nearly a hundred and fifty years and going back to long before the American Revolution. This he wished to have incorporated in his history:

Year	Sioux Name	Translation
1759	Wicableca han waniyetu	When they broke camp in winter
1760	Hokuwa wica kte pi	When they were killed where they were fishing
1761	Wanbli kuwa wica kte pi	They were killed while trapping eagles
1762	Pte ami wanpi	They swam toward the buffalo
1763	Mila wanica	When knives were not known
1764	Tajuskla kte pi	When Ant was killed
1765	Walagala kte pi	When Bag was killed
1766	Waze kute la ahi ktepi	Shooting Pines was killed
1767	Anub ob ivevipi	Help on both sides
1768	Iyeska kicizapi	Fought among themselves

Year	Sioux Name	Translation
1769	Ite han kiton kte pi	Wears Mask was killed
1770	Wakantanka knaskiye	The Great Spirit raved
1771	Miwatani oqu wicayapi	Set fire on the Mandans
1772	Canqnin yamni wica ktepi	Three killed when after wood
1773	Sunka ko ista miyapi	Dogs got snow blind
1774	Heyoka kagala ktepi	Acted-as-Clown was killed
1775	Payata i nonp wica ktepi	Two killed when went to a knoll
1776	Kiglala hi	Just Went came on visit
1777	Hohe ahi	The Assiniboins came
1778	Canaksay uha ktepi	Man-with-a-Club was killed
1779	Tukte' el wani tipi sni	Forgot the place of winter camp
1780	Slukela raka iwoto	Slukela put to death by magic
1781	Sunkawakan natan ahi	Horses came charging into camp
1782	Nawi-casli	When there were measles
1783	Sina luta in ktepi	Killed man who wore red blanket
1784	Akicita cuwitata	A soldier froze to death
1785	Oglala kin rante wan icupi	Ogalallas took a cedar
1786	Peici maza zyua ti	Iron Hair went into war camp
1787	Ohanzi atkuku ktepi	When Shade's father was killed
1788	Hoyoka kaga nonp wica ktepi	When Two-Clowns was killed
1789	Kangi ota tapi	When Many Crows perished
1790	Miwatani nonp carcoken weca ktepi	When they killed two Mandans in the middle of the ice
1791	Wowapi wan makokawinr yuha hi yayapi	When they went around the country with a flag
1792	Winyan wan ska wayakapi	When they saw a white woman
1793	Miwatani awicatipi	Camped to intercede for the Mandans

Year	Sioux Name	Translation
1794	Iteciqa wan ktepi	Killed a man with a small face
1795	Pehin hanskaska wan kte	Killed a man with long hair
1796	Miniyaye huya najin wan	Killed man standing in water vessel
1797	Wpaha katon wan ktepi	Killed man with war-bonnet on
1798	Wakantanka winyan wan eyeyapi	When found a woman Great Spirit
1799	Winyan iklusake ota tapi	Many pregnant women died
1800	Tacata sni wan ecun	Don't-Eat-Here performed magic
1801	Nawicas li	When they had measles
1802	Wasicu wan waste hi	When good white man came
1803	Sake maza awicaklipi	When they brought horses shod
1804	Sungugula awicaklipi	They brought curly horses
1805	Tasinte on akicilowanpi	When they had medicine song over one then another horse tail
1806	Sakilogan ahi wica ktepi	When eight were killed
1807	Wanbli kuwa eya wica ktepi	They killed the eagle trapper
1808	Okle luta on wan itkop ahi ktepi	Intercepted and killed man who wore a red shirt
1809	Sina to atkuku palani ahi	Blue Blanket's father killed by Cree
1810	Capa ciqa ti ile	Little Beaver's lodge burned
1811	Sinta wakaupi awicaklipi	Brought horses with feather in tails
1812	Palani top wica ktepi	When they killed four Rees
1813	Canka tanka atkuku palini	Bid Road's father killed by the Crees
1814	Witapahatu wan karugapi	A Kiowa clubbed to death

Year	*Sioux Name*	*Translation*
1815	Itazico ti tanka otipi	Has-No-Bows dwelt in a big lodge
1816	Ake okitipi	Again living in a big lodge
1817	Can sica om ticagapi	A building of dry branches
1818	Icasli nawicasli	When they had the measles
1819	Coze can punpun on Ticagepi	When they built with yellow wood
1820	Wan numblala wicicaske kicagapi	When Two-Arrows had a fastener of medicine
1821	Wicarpi wan hoton hiyaye ci	When the moving star sounded
1822	Waskula hu span	When Pealing froze his leg
1823	Wakmeza seca ots	When there was much bad corn
1824	Yeyela run ktepi	When Thrower was killed by magic
1825	Mini wicati	When people were drowned
1826	Kaiwayo klite	Kaiwayo came back dead
1827	Psa chanpi	When they boiled rushes
1828	Miwatani cta wica ktepi	Killed many Mandans
1829	Iteklegs wa aksija	When Spotted Face held the dead body he had killed
1830	Ptesan ota wica opi	Wounded many white buffalo cows
1831	Blestagu	When the lake burned
1832	Hewanjica Hu kawega	Lone Horn broke his leg
1833	Wicarpi okicamna	When the stars were shooting
1834	Sahivela ti kle wan ktepi	When a Cheyenne returning home was killed
1835	Tatanka wan cepa opi	When they wounded a fat buffalo bull
1836	Cara kicipi	Threw ice on them

Year	Sioux Name	Translation
1837	Itehepi sakiya tiapa ktepi	His-Face-Half-Red was killed
1838	Sunknaskinya cinca wan	Killed a mad pup
1839	Wicakiran watakpi ai	When starving he went to the attack
1840	Wakiyan ciqa sunkaka nonp wica kte	When Little Thunder killed two of his brothers
1841	Sunknapogi ota eye wica yapi	Found many brown-eared horses
1842	Wiyaka owin sunkyuha Najin wan kte	When Feather Ear-ring killed a lone horse herder
1843	Wiyaka aklipi	When they brought in captives
1844	Kangi bloka ahi ktepi	When they killed He-Crow
1845	Nawicasli	They had measles
1846	Susu ska wan ktepi	They killed White-Testicles
1847	Kengi wanbli capapa	They stabbed Crow-Eagle
1848	Winkte wan ktepi	They killed the hermaphrodite
1849	Nawicatipa	When they had cramps [cholera]
1850	Wicaranran	When they had smallpox
1851	Wakpamini	A big distribution [treaty]
1852	Wasma waniyetu	Winter of deep snow
1853	Mato wan wisan manu	When Bear raped a virgin
1854	Mato wayuhi ktepi	They killed Conquering-Bear
1855	Wicayajipa wa akaija	Hornet would not leave man he killed
1856	Kangiwicasa aksija	Crows met peacefully
1857	Kangi wicasa wikcemna wica	They killed ten Crows
1858	Tasina gi ktepi	When they killed Yellow-Blanket
1859	Kangi tanka ktepi	They killed Big-Crow

Year	Sioux Name	Translation
1860	Hoksicala tapi	When many babies died
1861	Sunkleska ktepi	They killed Spotted-Horse
1862	Hoksila wan waspapi	When they scalped a boy
1863	Saklogan ahi wica ktepi	When they killed eight
1864	Psa top wica ktepi	They killed eight Crows
1865	Sunk sotapi	When the horses died
1866	Wasicu opawinge wica ktepi	They killed one hundred white men
1867	Susuni tihi wan ktepi	Killed a Shoshone who came into camp
1868	Wakinyan heton irpeyapi	Thunder-Horn discarded [turned away]
1869	Winorcala wan can kate	Falling tree killed an old woman
1870	Canku wakantuya ahi ktepi	When they killed Big Breast
1871	Canrereka tain sni	When branches were crooked
1872	Anoka onae psa nonp wica kte	When Anus-on-Both-Sides killed two Crows
1873	Omaha nonp wica ktpe	Killed two Omahas
1874	Ehake ko wakantan si	Great Spirit made the last visit
1875	Waklure sakownin ahi aica ktp	They killed seven loafers
1876	Marpiya lute sunkipi	They took horses from Red Cloud (The U. S. Army did)
1877	Tasunka witko ktepi	When they killed Crazy Horse
1878	Sahiyela wakan wan ktpi	Cheyenne medicine man was killed
1879	Sunmanitu gleska ktpi	They killed Spotted Wolf
1880	Susu gleska ktepi	Killed Spotted Testicles
1881	Sinta gleska ktepi	When they killed Spotted Tail

Year	Sioux Name	Translation
1882	Cancaga cinca wan kte	Drum's son committed suicide
1883	Ite canogu tahu pawega	Burnt Face broke his neck
1884	Tatanka ska tawicu kikte	White Bull killed his wife
1885	Peta wicasa wan irpeyepi	Banished the fire-man
1886	Yuptanyan wanu ktepi	Turn-Over was accidentally killed
1887	Wakan wanu ktepi	Holy Wolf accidentally killed
1888	Waparta yublacapi	When the pack was undone
1889	Okle sa tankasitku wan ici	Red Shirt's sister suicided
1890	Si-tanka ktepi	When they killed Big Foot
1891	Maka mani akcita wica kagapi	They enlisted walking soldiers
1892	Can nonp yuha pte eya wica kt	Has-Two-Sticks killed cattle herder
1893	Owayawa tanka ile	The big school burned
1894	Can nonp yuha pa nakee yapi	Hanged Has-Two-Sticks
1895	Hoka omniciye tanka kagapi	First big Council held
1896	Tintkala ska tawaniyetu	When White Bird died
1897	Talo tipi ile	The meat house burned
1898	Toka cankaske kagapi	When they made the fence
1899	Petaga tawaniyetu	Makes-fires year
1900	Wakpamni netakapi	Distribution stopped
1901	Wicaranran	The year of the smallpox
1902	Winorcala wna tainani	When Old-Woman disappeared
1903	Tarca kute eya wica ktp	They killed the deer-hunters
1904	Toka makiyutapi waniyetu	When allotment began
1905	Wapaha rota wan icinti	Gray Hat's son committed suicide
1906	Toka pts maka olutapi	Reservation leased to cattlemen

It is unfortunate that the calendar ceases at 1906. It would be interesting to know how they recorded the World War fighting and their comments on the many of their race and tribe sent to Europe to fight for the white man's claims against a foreign nation.

INDEX

Index

$\mathcal{F}$IREWATER AND FORKED TONGUES
has been composed on the Linotype in Baskerville type and
printed on Monastery Text book paper, 60 pound substance,
on the presses of MURRAY & GEE, INC., Culver City,
California. ¶ Title-page and typography by MARVIN
MILLER. ¶ Proofreading and indexing by CORNELIA
N. COOK. ¶ Book jacket lithographed by HOMER H.
BOELTER, Los Angeles, California. ¶ Original
water color painting of Flying Hawk on book
jacket by JOE SCHEUERLE. ¶ Drawing of
broken arrow by CLARENCE ELLSWORTH.
End paper illustration from drawing by
CHARLES M. RUSSELL. ¶ Engravings
by METROPOLITAN ENGRAVERS, Los
Angeles, California. ¶ Binding
by WEBER-McCREA, INC., Los
Angeles, California.

CPSIA information can be obtained
at www.ICGtesting.com
Printed in the USA
BVHW041529090819
555498BV00002B/183/P